Common Threads

My Family's Journey from Slave Owner to Abolitionist

By Ben A. Jobe

A WRITEWAY Book

Copyright 2013 by Ben A. Jobe

Scripture taken from the NEW AMERICAN STANDARD BIBLE, c 1960, 1962, 1963, 1968, 1971, 1972, 1973, 1975, 1977 by the Lockman Foundation. Used by permission.

All rights reserved.

ISBN: 0615745253
ISBN 13: 9780615745251
Library of Congress Control Number: 2013939011
CreateSpace Independent Publishing Platform
North Charleston, South Carolina

Contents

PROLOGUE: The Horrible Cost of Courage 1

FOREWORD 5

PART ONE: Ancestral Threads 9
    Making a Life after the War 17

PART TWO: Paris Patterns 23
    Times of Want and Times of Plenty 31
    Segregation Out! 39

PART THREE: Family Fabric 49
    Mom's Family: Grays, Halls, Durhams, and Hurds 63
    Newlyweds in Wartime 71
    Peacetime Baby Boom 75
    Middle Tennessee Grandma 81
    No Place Like Home 85
    Music and Words 95
    Out West and Home Again 101
    Saving Howard & Jobe 105
    Band and Paper Days 111
    Sister Story 115
    Retirement and Beyond 121

PART FOUR: My Own Weave 127
    A Time to Kill and a Time to Heal 133
    Mr. Cool 149

More Madness	153
Music City Ups and Downs	157
Atlanta's Siren Song	163
Big Changes	169

PART FIVE: Tennessee Tapestry 177

Family Destruction	181
Divine Sunshine	185
South of the Border	191
Love Song	197
Here Comes the Professor	203
New Millennium, New Faces	211

PART SIX: Cloth of Many Colors 219

Two Ben Jobes	223
Ending Slavery Today	229

EPILOGUE: The Fabric of Freedom 237

About the Author 241

Acknowledgments

Many people have graciously contributed to this project. First, I wish to thank my friend Coach Ben Jobe of Montgomery, Alabama, without whose help and encouragement this would never have happened. In my hometown Paris, Tennessee, Jim Tubbs and Leon and Bradley Ridgeway helped with research.

In the Nashville area where I live, the list is even longer: Professor Len Assante, Eric Melcher, and Tami Wallace of Volunteer State Community College in Gallatin; Professors Elizabeth White and Dr. Judith Russell of Motlow State Community College in Smyrna; Volunteer State 2011 graduate Jamie Blurton, Karen Karpinski, and Derri Smith, all of End Slavery Tennessee; and Dr. Steve Bond of Broadman & Holman Publishers. Special thanks to Andy Raines for technical help.

I am especially grateful to family members Marilyn Hendricks, Bill Jobe, Joshua Jobe, and John Moore. Some material about our family's past is from a document compiled in the 1960s by the late Mary Jobe Cannon and

Mary Jobe Pillow. The section on my mother's family was compiled by her.

Details about my great-grandfather Ben Avant Jobe's service in the Civil War are from a letter he wrote to the Confederate Pension Board in Nashville around 1905 seeking a pension, which he never received! I also wish to thank the Sam Davis Home and Museum in Smyrna, Tennessee, for granting permission to photograph DeWitt Smith Jobe memorabilia.

*Dedicated to my parents—
Ben Anderson Jobe, Sr. (1906–1999)
And Mary Alice Hall Jobe (1918–1995)*

A portion of the proceeds from this book will go to
End Slavery Tennessee

Prologue:

The Horrible Cost of Courage

The young man had ridden hard all day and into the night, trying to get home. Travel by day was dangerous. At night, it was easier to cover your tracks. Only a few miles from home, he couldn't go any farther. Exhausted, he stopped and asked permission to sleep in a cornfield. He gladly savored a few hours' rest under the starry summer sky.

But early the next morning, he heard them coming through the rows of lush, green ripe corn. He quickly tore the message he carried into thin strips, chewed them up and swallowed them. He was almost finished when he was surrounded by fifteen soldiers in bright blue uniforms. The sun glinted off their weapons as they closed ranks around him.

"Well, well, Reb!" one of them said. "What do you have to say for yourself?"

"What are you eating, Reb? Is that your breakfast?" Several of them laughed but the young man said nothing, looking at his captors in disgust.

"Tell us what was in that message!"

The young man remained silent.

"Tie him up, boys!" their commander ordered. "Make him talk!"

The young man just stared at a distant place only he could see. Someone hit him in the mouth with his rifle butt. Another soldier followed his lead. After several blows, the young man's mouth was bloody and missing some teeth.

"Come on now, Reb! We don't have all day!"

"Make it easy on yourself," another solider urged him.

But the young man kept his thousand-yard stare.

A soldier unsheathed his big shiny knife. "I know how to make him talk."

He gouged out one of their captive's eyes, then the other!

The young man screamed curses at them!

Someone else grasped his knife, forced open their prisoner's mouth and as another soldier held his head, cut out the young man's tongue!

A piece of paper and a pencil were shoved at him.

"This is your last chance! Write down the message! Do it now!"

The young man's face and clothing were covered in his blood, but he never wavered in his resolve.

"Well, that's it, Reb! Too bad you didn't talk; would have made it so much easier!"

A leather strap was tied around the young man's neck and the other end to a horse. The horse was lashed and ran off, pulling the dying man behind it. One of the enemy soldiers said after the young man died, that he was "the bravest man I've ever seen!"

News of this crime spread quickly. After the soldiers had gone, a woman passing by who knew the dead man's family, stopped and covered his face with her handkerchief.

Word reached the young man's home a few miles away. A slave named Frank was sent with a horse and wagon to get the body. When he returned home, Frank and his brother Scott began one of the toughest jobs of their lives: making the dead man's coffin. Their owner had a furniture shop and was especially renowned for his coffins.

The dead man was DeWitt Smith Jobe (1840–1864), a member of Coleman's Scouts serving the Confederate Army of Tennessee. He died on Monday, August 29, 1864, near Nolensville, Tennessee, a Nashville suburb today.

DeWitt's father was Elihu Coleman Jobe (1809–1892), who owned Frank and Scott. The family farm and furniture shop were near present-day Smyrna, Tennessee. DeWitt's older brother was Ben Avant Jobe (1837–1928), my great-grandfather. I am a college professor in the Nashville area and a latter-day abolitionist. Since 2009 I have been a volunteer with End Slavery Tennessee, which fights human trafficking: modern-day slavery.

Join me on a journey through a century and a half and five generations— from slavery in my own family to modern-day slavery and the growing abolitionist movement. I will do my best to make the trip worthwhile and I will show you "common threads" that connect it all.

Foreword

"May You Live in Interesting Times"

- Chinese Proverb

On a Monday in April, 2008, I received two phone calls the same day for a mysterious man whom I had never met but had heard about for many years, because we share the same first and last names. This other Ben Jobe was a well-known college basketball coach. The callers were both former players. The calls were ripple effects from *"Black Magic,"* a documentary that had aired the previous Sunday on ESPN.

I asked one of the callers, when he found the right Ben Jobe, to please have him call me. That evening the phone rang and it was Coach Ben. We later met and have since become good friends. Ben and I sometimes call each other "Brother" and there is some truth to that.

Coach Ben and I have a family connection going back to slavery days. We have pieced together information from our respective families that my great great-grandfather Elihu Coleman Jobe (1809–1892), a farmer and furniture maker in Rutherford County, Tennessee, once owned Coach Ben's grandfather Scott and his great- great-uncle Frank Jobe. The two brothers were skilled craftsmen who fashioned furniture in his shop on the family farm near Smyrna.

Ironically, I have taught classes at Motlow State Community College in Smyrna since 2000. Some of the legwork for making these connections was done by my cousin John Moore, a Smyrna resident.

What is amazing about this story, besides being true, is how much Coach Ben Jobe and I have in common. We are both teachers at heart. We both love learning. In fact, Coach Ben and I rarely talk basketball. But we have much in common besides that.

I always look forward to seeing him. His job for the New York Knicks brings him to Nashville from time to time. We hang out and I have even become something of a basketball fan thanks to him.

Some might question how the descendant of a slave owner and the descendant of one of his slaves might have any basis for friendship. For me, it's not that hard to figure out. Coach Ben and I share a common heritage, a "common thread." We believe it is a story worth telling.

The civil-rights movement changed America and the world. In a very small way, my family was part of that: employing Dave Travis so he could lead the local NAACP without fear of being fired; my mother introducing me to Sidney Poitier's work in films; my sister sharing a classroom with Wilson Kendall, whose mother worked for our family business. And my parents always leading by example as they taught us how to get along with everyone.

These were not dramatic, world-shaking events. But they helped to shape my worldview and open my mind to new possibilities. I think our family was typical of millions of others in the South, black and white, who shared a simple, decent desire to get along with each other despite the barriers imposed by segregation. That is one of many "common threads."

Ben Jobe
Nashville, Tennessee
July 2012

Part One:

Ancestral Threads

"There is an appointed time for everything...a time for every purpose under heaven"

(Ecclesiastes 3:1).

Our thread in the Jobe family tapestry began when a Revolutionary War veteran named James Jobe came to Tennessee from Virginia (date unknown). He married Catherine Pitt from North Carolina, apparently after moving to Tennessee. James died in Maury County in 1833. He and Catherine raised five children.

Elihu Coleman Jobe, one of their three sons, was born on August 9, 1809, in Maury County. He married Mary Smith. They settled in Rutherford County near present-day Smyrna. Elihu and Mary had seven children—three sons and four daughters. Their second son was my great-grandfather, Ben Avant Jobe (1837–1928). Elihu also owned two slaves, Frank and Scott Jobe

In 1858, Ben was hired as the bookkeeper for a plantation in Mississippi. To get there, he rode his horse down the Natchez Trace from Nashville (the same route the Natchez Trace Parkway follows today), where he served for two years.

By 1860, Ben was getting homesick. Even though his employer was pleased with his work and offered him a substantial raise to stay on, my great grandfather decided to return home. He arrived back in Rutherford County not long before the war began that would change the lives of the entire family, including their two slaves, Frank and Scott.

During the Civil War, my great-grandfather enlisted in the Eighteenth Tennessee Infantry of the Confederate army. In February, 1862, he was captured at Fort Donelson, near Dover, Tennessee, after a four-day battle in the freezing cold. He contracted pneumonia and was taken to a federal hospital in St. Louis where he spent several weeks.

Ben recovered, took an amnesty oath, and was released. He returned to Tennessee and served in the Fourth Division of the Tennessee Cavalry under Nathan Bedford Forrest. (Forrest is remembered today for being a military genius during the Civil War.) Ben was selected as a member of Wharton's Scouts and promoted to lieutenant.

He was captured again in Shelbyville, Tennessee and escaped just hours before he was to be hanged. The Shelbyville escape was particularly daring. Great-Grandfather was chained to a bed in the upstairs of a store, under guard. While the guard was not paying attention, Ben tore open a feather pillow, stuck a feather down his throat and made himself sick!

Behind the store was a creek. Ben asked the guard if he could bathe his face in the water. The guard agreed. With hands still chained, Ben reached down into the water. There was enough moonlight he could see well enough to find a large rock. He grabbed the rock, sprang up and hit the guard on the head, knocking him out! Ben took his keys, freed himself, and ran away!

My great-grandfather also escaped after a third and final capture early in 1865. This happened while his horse was being shod at a blacksmith in Helena, Arkansas. During the struggle, a bullet passed through his hat, but did not touch him!

Ben was put on a barge loaded with cotton at Memphis. The final destination was a federal prison at Rock Island, Illinois. The barge stopped at Tiptonville, Tennessee, late one cold winter afternoon. Ben and the other prisoners were forced to load more cotton. Ben slipped away in the gathering darkness.

He tried to reenter the war several times, traveling as far north as Metropolis, Illinois, across the Ohio River from Paducah, Kentucky, to no avail. The war would end soon anyway. Ben returned to his new bride, Julia, whom he had married on Christmas Eve, 1864, in northern Henry County, Tennessee. Julia Pillow Jobe was the daughter of Mary Pitt Jobe Pillow, Elihu's sister. She was thus my great-grandfather's first cousin.

Elihu had Frank and Scott make a chest of drawers for the new couple as a wedding present. That antique chest is in the dining room of our Nashville home today. In the same room is a child's high chair, also made in the furniture shop.

Elihu's third son, DeWitt Smith Jobe (1840–1864) became a hero in the Civil War. He was a member of Coleman's Scouts, serving the Confederate Army of Tennessee. On August 29, 1864, DeWitt was captured by fifteen Union soldiers. When he refused to give information he had after prolonged torture, including having his tongue cut off and eyes gouged out, the soldiers tied a leather strap around his neck. The strap was tied to a horse and he was dragged to his death.

Tragically, Dewitt was only a few miles from home when he was captured. He stopped to rest after having ridden all the way from Chattanooga. Exhausted, he made the fatal mistake of sleeping in a field whose owner he knew. Being a polite Southern gentleman, DeWitt Jobe asked permission before bedding down. The

Yankees were later told his whereabouts and found him early the next morning.

My father told me that DeWitt, a handsome twenty-four-year-old when he died, had recently broken up with his girlfriend for another lady. The man who owned the field where DeWitt spent his last night was the ex- girlfriend's father! Did he betray DeWitt?

When news of DeWitt's death reached the Jobe family farm on Rocky Fork Road near Smyrna, where Coach Ben Jobe's ancestors Scott and Frank were slaves, Elihu sent Frank to get DeWitt's body. Later, the two black Jobes had the sad duty of making DeWitt's coffin!

There is a story about his first cousin, Dee Smith, who when he heard of his Jobe cousin's death, became "unhinged" and "ran up the black flag"—a symbol of death—vowing to kill as many Yankees as possible. Dee Smith quietly slipped into tents of various Union soldiers by night and slit their throats with a butcher knife. No one knows exactly how many he killed before being captured and executed himself.

Historical markers at Nolensville and Smyrna, Tennessee (both near Nashville), commemorate the tragic demise of DeWitt Smith Jobe. The Smyrna marker is more recent and includes his photograph. It is part of the Civil War Trails series.

In 1965, the *Nashville Banner* (Nashville's afternoon newspaper at the time) published a commemorative book on the Civil War in Middle Tennessee. Staff writer

Ed Huddleston, who put the project together, dedicated the book to DeWitt Smith Jobe, believing him to be the unsung hero who most deserved recognition.

Elihu's daughter Martha Ann's descendant is my Smyrna cousin John Moore, who has played a key role in this story. John took part in placing a cast-iron marker over DeWitt's grave with the Sons of Confederate Veterans. Our hero is buried on a hill near the site of the old family farm near Smyrna. I have seen the grave with the marker. I also own DeWitt Smith Jobe's hunting horn.

Ben Avant Jobe returned to Julia in northern Henry County, Tennessee, to begin starting a family and making a life in the post-Civil War South. My great-grandfather lived a long, full life, finally passing away in 1928 at the age of ninety-one. When he died, he was a great-grandfather to my cousin Jean, who was born in 1927.

One of his grandchildren was my father, Ben Anderson Jobe, Sr. I'm sure he spent many happy hours telling Dad and my uncle Howard about his Civil War adventures, especially his many miraculous escapes. The thread of his life touched four generations and bound us together in a distinctive family fabric.

Top Left/Right: Elihu C. Jobe farmhouse(1860?), near Smyrna, TN/ DeWitt Smith Jobe(1840-64), in uniform.
Center Left/Right: Original Road Marker (1969)/ Civil War Trails Marker, near depot, downtown Smyrna, TN.
Lowest Left/Middle/Right: Award Certificate / Plaque / Medal of Honor, Sam Davis Museum, Smyrna, TN.
Photos taken and sketch drawn, by John Moore
Photos taken, by permission, of The Sam Davis Museum, Smyrna, TN

Making a Life after the War

Ben and Julia had four children:
- DeWitt Smith Jobe, born March 5, 1865, and died February 16, 1872
- Horace Elbert Jobe, born August 22, 1868, and died November 5, 1953.
- Florence Jobe, born February 14, 1872, and died February 22, 1949
- Mary Jobe Pillow, born March 14, 1875, and died in 1969.

DeWitt Smith Jobe, named for his uncle who had died a hero's death during the Civil War, also died tragically. On February 16, 1872, just two days after his sister Florence had been born, the child, who was almost seven at the time, was sitting in a buggy waiting for his grandmother Pillow to take him home with her.

Suddenly, the horse became frightened and ran away. He was thrown from the buggy and killed instantly. My grandfather Horace, who was just three-and-a-half years old, saw it all.

Horace grew into a strong young man, but he did not take to farm life. He attended school through the sixth grade, which was typical of the times. But when he was eighteen, my grandfather left home for Paris, Tennessee, the county seat about ten miles south. His life would not be in the soil, but in commerce.

Puryear, the rural community where they lived, was on a railroad to Paris, Tennessee, which was also on the main line of the Louisville and Nashville Railroad (now part of the CSX system) between Memphis and Louisville.

It took a steam locomotive three days to travel between the two cities. Paris was at the end of a day's run, a division point. The railroad had large shops there to repair and maintain rolling stock. The shops were the town's largest employer. Paris had a lot more opportunities than Puryear.

By the turn of the century, Paris even had a music hall—the Crete Opera House—a block off the courthouse square beside one set of tracks that ran through downtown. Touring shows had to stop for the night. The Opera House was right across the street from a fine hotel and across the tracks from another.

In 1975, I interviewed a lady in a nursing home for a video project at nearby Murray State University (Murray, Kentucky) where I was a graduate student in communications. She said her father had taken her to the Opera House to see the stage play *Ben-Hur* when she was seven years old.

There were real horses on the stage for the chariot race, running on treadmills. It had been a hot summer night and she remembered how the pungent horse aroma permeated the hall. It must have been something to see, hear, and smell!

My grandfather was hired by a large dry-goods store on the square called Head & Carter. Besides working there during the day, his job included being their "night security man." The store was in a three-story building. Horace stayed in a small furnished room on the top floor. While he had an incredibly short commute to work, he could leave only on Sunday, his only day off.

Many Sundays after church, he would catch the train to Puryear, visit his family in the afternoon, then return to Paris on a later train that evening for another week at the store. He worked there for twelve years, until he was thirty. By then, he had the hands-on equivalent of a college degree in retailing.

We are not sure how or when Horace met Inez Howard, but I have always suspected it was through her father Joseph Howard's general store, which was also in downtown Paris.

Joseph W. Howard, Sr. (1837–-1923), was also a Civil War veteran like Ben Avant Jobe. He had been wounded in the Battle of Atlanta in 1864. There is a famous scene in the film *"Gone With the Wind"* showing thousands of wounded Confederate soldiers lying out in the rail yards in the blazing August sun. My great-grandfather Howard was one of these men!

Great-Grandpa Howard had a taken a bullet in the leg. The bullet had been removed. I doubt they used an anesthetic! (My father told me of childhood visits to his grandfather Howard on Sunday afternoons where, after a little coaxing, he would roll up his pant leg and show all the admiring children his bullet hole. It probably made their day!)

J. W. Howard lay out in that Atlanta rail yard for several days until a woman came by with a mule and wagon and put him and another wounded man into it. She had lost both her husband and son in the war. The woman, whose name we do not know, took Howard and the other man, who was from Milan, Tennessee, to her farm outside Atlanta. Her kindness saved their lives. It was a thread of mercy that profoundly affected our family tapestry.

After they recovered, the woman gave the men her mule, which they took turns riding back to Tennessee. They reached a crossroads between Paris and Milan and flipped a coin to see who would get the mule. Howard won the toss. When he got home to Henry County, he used the mule to plant his first crop in the spring of 1865.

Years later, J. W. Howard opened his general store in Paris. He married and had a family. One of his daughters, Inez (1874–1951), became the object of Horace's affections. Apparently, the feeling was mutual. On April 26, 1900, they were married.

On January 1, 1901, another "marriage" took place. Joseph Howard and his new son-in-law founded Howard & Jobe. Howard's expertise had been in retailing items needed by farmers such as seed, animal feed, tools, and the like.

Horace's years with the dry-goods firm had given him knowledge of the piece-goods business. In those days, there were few ready-to-wear clothes. Most people in places like Paris, Tennessee, bought cloth and made their clothes at home by hand or with a sewing machine.

Howard and Jobe combined their respective business backgrounds to form Howard & Jobe. The combined retail enterprise would grow as Paris grew, survive the Depression, two World Wars, and almost the entire twentieth century. The store's birth year 1901 began that new century and Howard & Jobe was poised to make the most of it: a thread of commerce that would last almost another century.

Part Two:

Paris Patterns

"The Lord is my Shepherd; I shall not want"

(Psalm 23:1).

Paris, Tennessee, in the early twentieth century, was a land of opportunity for young men like Horace Jobe. The new firm he and his father-in-law had founded could serve the needs of farmers and townspeople as well. The store sold such items as ladies' hats and horse collars, piece goods by the yard and animal feed by the bushel, plus a lot of other things in between. It was a good combination for success.

My father even told me that in the store's first years, there was a chicken coop behind the building (in downtown Paris!) to house live chickens given by customers in trade.

This bartering was still practiced in the early twentieth century in rural Tennessee. As time passed, the chicken coop succumbed to progress in the form of cash, credit, and finally credit cards.

January, 1901 was a huge milestone in Horace's business and personal life. On January 20, Inez gave birth to their first child, a son named William Howard Jobe. My uncle grew into an astute merchant, tutored by his father. He graduated from Grove High School in 1919. By then, he had already begun his retail career.

Howard spent most of his adult life in the family business, eventually becoming a partner. In 1961, after suffering a stroke, he sold his interest in the business to my parents, who became the sole owners. Howard died in 1979.

In March, 1926, Uncle Howard had married Mary Lee Morris (d. 1980) of Big Sandy, Tennessee. They had two children, my cousins Mary Jean (1927–2002) and William Howard, Jr., born December 10, 1928.

As of 2012, my cousin Bill was living in Harlingen, Texas, as a retired teacher and guidance counselor. He served four years in the navy in the early 1950s, following his graduation from Baylor University in Waco, Texas. After working at Howard & Jobe for several years and teaching one year in Florida, he returned to Texas in 1960 and earned his master's and later his specialist in education degrees.

When I was a child, Cousin Bill would take me for rides in his 1948 light green Buick convertible Grandpa Horace had bought him for college. I had never ridden in a cloth-top convertible before and was enthralled! I thought my older cousin was so cool!

Jean also graduated from Baylor University. She received her master's in education from George Peabody College for Teachers (now part of Vanderbilt University) in Nashville. She married Captain (later Colonel) Howard Lynn Strohecker in June, 1953.

He was a West Point graduate and was in the Army Corps of Engineers. "Bud" was originally from Portland, Oregon. He died in 2002, three months before Jean. They had three sons, two of whom are still living.

On October 19, 1906, Horace and Inez became parents again when my father Ben Anderson Jobe, Sr., was born. The middle name had not been in our family line. In 1901, when Howard & Jobe began, Horace had been doing business with a wholesale dry-goods firm in Cincinnati, Ohio, through a Mr. Anderson.

Anderson generously offered Howard & Jobe a credit line of $1,000 to stock their new firm with inventory. This was a considerable sum of money in those days, but Howard & Jobe was able to pay the loan back by the end of the year.

In 1906, Grove High School was also born, one of few public high schools in the nation to be privately endowed. The school was founded with a gift of $80,000 from Edwin Wiley Grove, a Paris pharmacist who had become rich from a "tasteless chill tonic" he had developed for malaria in the 1880s.

Grove founded the Paris Medicine Co. to manufacture his tonic in 1886. It sold so well, a few years later he moved the business to St. Louis as Grove Laboratories. The firm was later sold to pharmaceutical giant Bristol-Myers.

My cousin Bill remembers being given "tasteless chill tonic" as a child! We have a bottle of it in a cabinet in our home with other family memorabilia.

E. W. Grove High School's first classes met in the county courthouse in the fall of 1906. Construction began on the Tower Building, on top of what was dubbed "Grove Hill." A bottle of "tasteless chill tonic" was placed in the cornerstone. The building looked like a European castle. For many education-minded Parisians, it was a citadel of knowledge, a fortress of learning!

When the Tower Building was completed, classes moved there, to be followed by other buildings in later decades. Perched on top of Grove Hill with a commanding view of downtown Paris, the campus resembled a college more than a high school. By 1958, Grove Junior High had been added to the complex. I attended eighth and ninth grades there.

Members of our family who graduated from Grove High include Uncle Howard in 1919, my father in 1924, and my cousins Jean and Bill in 1945 and 1946, respectively. My turn came in 1963, followed by my sister Marilyn in 1967. Mom taught senior English there from 1958 until 1962, when she became a partner with my dad at Howard & Jobe. Grove High School was an important educational thread in the life of our community and our family.

As the first decade of the century moved into the second, Paris was growing and Howard & Jobe along with it. J. W. Howard had been sixty-four years old when the firm was founded in 1901. As he grew older, he became less active in the business. Joe Howard, Sr., died in 1923.

As Howard & Jobe forged ahead, attempting to keep pace with changing times and market conditions, farm goods took a back seat to "fine fashion for men and women." Much of this direction was established by Uncle Howard. He wanted Howard & Jobe to be known as the "most expensive store in town!"

By the early 1920s, Howard & Jobe was almost exclusively a Jobe family business. Paris was becoming more "uptown," in a small-town way of course. The store began to carry items of ready-made clothing as well as the piece goods Horace had learned about at Head & Carter as a young man.

They also stocked shoes, which were my father's special love. He knew the shoe sizes of many of his customers. Dad would often read an obituary in the local newspaper and say, "He wore a seven-and-a-half C!" or whatever the size was. Talk about a man who loved his work!

By the post-World War II era, my early lifetime, Howard & Jobe carried such merchandise as ladies' lingerie, hosiery, purses, scarves, and other accessories, plus men's dress shirts, ties, socks, wallets, belts, hats, and tailored suits, specially ordered from Cincinnati.

One thing that made Grandpa Horace a successful businessman was his attention to detail. This went beyond just minding the store. He read a lot, including *The Commercial Appeal,* the daily newspaper from Memphis, which came to Paris on the L & N.

One day early in 1919, shortly after World War I had ended, Horace noticed a small item in the Memphis paper's business section: a textile mill in Massachusetts was laying off all five thousand of its workers and closing due to dramatically falling demand for its products.

The next week, when the piece-goods salesman came by to take orders, Horace cut his usual order in half! He did this again the following week. The salesman was irate, of course, but Horace could be immovable once he made a decision! Time proved him right.

Other Paris stores did not change their buying patterns. Over the next several weeks, all of them except Howard & Jobe accumulated large surpluses of piece-goods inventory. The demand for piece goods stayed low for a long time. After two or three years, most of

Howard & Jobe's retail competitors had gone out of business.

Grandpa owned several automobiles. I remember a 1939 gray Pontiac four-door sedan. He kept that car until he died in 1953. However, he never learned to drive any of them. In his later years, he had his employee, a black man named Dave Travis, drive him around town in the Pontiac.

Some people thought the Jobes had much more money than we did because of this. But the "chauffeur" was only because Grandfather had never learned to drive! Instead of "Driving Miss Daisy," it was "Driving Mr. Horace."

In 1927, Howard & Jobe, which had been on the south side of the square on Wood Street, moved to a two-story building in the center of the block at 108 North Market Street, on the west side of the courthouse. Horace had bought the building. Howard & Jobe would stay in this location until it finally closed its doors in 1997.

This building apparently had a colorful history prior to becoming the home of our family retail store. On the back outside wall, which opened onto an alley, you could see the word "SALOON" in faded paint.

The S-word stayed there even after the remodeling of 1950–-51. Perhaps because it was on the rear of the building, it was simply not considered important enough to remove. Later, in the 1960s, the "SALOON" was painted into oblivion.

The upstairs still bore traces of separate rooms, which at one time might have been used for offices or even bedrooms! One can only imagine what might have happened there before it became Howard & Jobe's home in 1927. If those walls could talk, they might have spun many fascinating threads from the past.

Times of Want and Times of Plenty

In October, 1929, an economic tsunami began on Wall Street in New York City, the stock-market crash, which eventually impacted Paris. This tidal wave grew into the Great Depression. The "Roaring Twenties" were history!

My father, Uncle Howard, and their father, Horace, bravely steered their store through our nation's worst economic storm. Through careful management of resources and prayer, the family business survived. But things were tough for several years. My father told me in the early 1930s they could not afford any clerks! It was a family business, literally!

Henry County suffered along with the rest of Tennessee and the nation. Many left to seek work elsewhere.

During the Depression, the railroads, especially the Louisville & Nashville shops, were an economic lifeline for many families.

However, the shops offered only seasonal employment—about seven or eight months of the year. During spring and summer they laid people off in droves. Most men who worked for the L & N shops farmed or did odd jobs to make ends meet.

When Franklin D. Roosevelt was elected president in 1932, promising a "New Deal" for the nation, many Parisians, including my family, hoped and prayed it would happen. Would "Happy Days" come here again?

One landmark piece of legislation the New Deal birthed was the Tennessee Valley Authority (TVA), which benefited the vast Tennessee Valley covering parts of several states. As late as 1940, a majority of homes in Henry County, along with the Valley in general, were heated by either coal- or wood-burning stoves. Rural areas usually did not have electricity. Fortunately, Paris did, though not all could afford it.

The lack of rural electricity may have helped Saturday business in the early years of Howard & Jobe. Many country people came to town to shop and visit. Howard & Jobe, like most downtown stores, had electric lights and was open late, sometimes until 9:00 p.m. or later.

Folks dropped by the store to enjoy the rare experience of electric lighting. If they saw a friend or relative, they might visit for extended periods. The store's late hours were often determined by its customers! Of course, many bought things, so it all paid off in the end. I was often taught, "The customer is ALWAYS right!"

I remember many people I personally waited on at the store (where I worked as a teenager in the early 1960s and later as a graduate student in the mid-1970s) telling me how their parents and grandparents had shopped there! Apparently, shopping at Howard & Jobe became a family tradition for some.

As TVA built dams across the vast Tennessee Valley region, affordable electric power came to farms and towns alike. Henry County's turn came when Kentucky Dam was built in western Kentucky in 1944. By the end of World War II, everyone in the county who wanted it could have affordable electricity.

The Second World War was a time of death and destruction for Europe and Japan and for many American families as well. But for Paris and Henry County, it was a time of prosperity fueled by the demands of the overseas conflict.

In the southwestern part of the county, a large army base was built, Camp Tyson. (It closed after the war.) This brought an influx of new people, most of them from outside the region. Some stayed on after the war by choice.

Our neighbors during my childhood were the Lonardos. Tom Lonardo was originally from Rhode Island, and was brought to Camp Tyson by the war. He married a young local woman and stayed in Paris the rest of his life.

Mr. Lonardo was a professional musician. He had a "big band." They played swing music, which was so popular during that era. He also owned a music store. I still have sheet music from the Tom Lonardo Piano Co.

The wartime population of Paris swelled to twelve thousand, more people than live there now. (The 2010 Census population was 10, 156.) Homes for officers and their families were built in a fine residential area east of downtown. The highway between Paris and the base—US 79—was improved and in town was called Tyson Avenue. Servicemen traveled in and out of Paris by train so there was a lot of activity downtown. Howard & Jobe's most profitable years were during this period.

When the war ended in 1945, the year I was born, Paris, the state, the nation, and the world were all changed forever. The war brought peace, but in a few years something sinister called the Cold War developed with the Soviet Union, our former ally against Nazi Germany.

I remember fallout shelters and "drills" in school where we were told to hide under our desks! This was during the 1950s, which today many believe to have been a time of innocence of the kind portrayed in the 1970s television show *"Happy Days."*

The year 1951 was a milestone for Howard & Jobe—the store's fiftieth anniversary. Horace and his two sons engineered a complete remodeling of the store property to give the business a more modern look. The exterior and interior were given an ambitious upgrade. The new, large plate-glass show windows reflected the post-war euphoria that Paris shared with the rest of the nation.

By now, our store was air-conditioned. Howard & Jobe had purchased a unit that was war surplus, installed in 1947. It had been used on a navy ship and had lots of excess capacity. Because it was never utilized to its full extent, this air-conditioning unit lasted until the 1970s! It served longer on land than at sea!

Industry grew dramatically. In 1948, Paris became the site of Holley Carburetor Co., later a part of Colt Industries. This plant at one time employed more than one thousand people and lasted until the mid-1980s.

Other major industries came to town in the 1950s and '60s: Emerson Electric, Midland-Ross, Tecumseh and Plumley (acquired by Dana Corp.), to name some of the largest. At least two of these were suppliers to the automotive industry.

This industrial growth came as the railroads began a period of decline after the war. The L & N shops eventually closed. But their pool of skilled labor helped Paris get other, better-paying industries.

For decades, Paris was also home to the cosmetics industry. The largest firm was Golden Peacock, which was later bought by Revlon. My father told me about another local cosmetics firm that put on all its products' packaging the words "Made in Paris."

Of course, most American consumers assumed the item came from Paris, France! Dad said the Federal Trade Commission heard about this and made the company stop their deceptive labeling.

Paris in recent years has capitalized on being the namesake of the French capital. There is a metal replica of the Eiffel Tower in one municipal park. It is much smaller than the original—only about sixty feet tall! There are also Eiffel Towers painted on storefronts and signs, especially in the highway corridor toward Paris Landing State Park on Kentucky Lake.

The park was begun in 1949, just a few years after the formation of Kentucky Lake, most of which is actually in Tennessee. (There have been many proposals by loyal Tennesseans to change the lake's name!)

In fact, the land between Paris and the lake has in recent years grown to be a haven for retirees. It is hilly and wooded. This natural beauty close to the huge lake has attracted many new residents. Kentucky Lake is believed to be the largest manmade lake by surface area east of the Mississippi.

In 1954, the Paris-Henry County Chamber of Commerce began an annual celebration to capitalize on the town's proximity to the lake—the World's Biggest Fish Fry. They still have this festival the last weekend of April. It has put Paris, Tennessee, on the map.

There are parades, beauty contests, a fishing rodeo, and lots of deep-fried catfish-and-hushpuppy dinners.

I was a drummer in the Grove High School band in the early 1960s. We marched in every Fish Fish parade, which was always on Friday. Schools were closed as it was a holiday. I looked forward to the Fish Fry every year.

Also, in 1953, a new, large medical facility opened on Tyson Avenue: Henry County General Hospital. It was four stories tall and much better equipped than Nobles, which eventually closed. Henry County Medical Center, as it is now known, has dominated the local healthcare scene ever since.

Many of these new postwar developments were not open to everyone. Paris Landing State Park and most other Tennessee state parks were for whites only! There were two state parks—-one near Memphis and another near Chattanooga—-for African-Americans. As I grew aware of all this, I sometimes wondered where black people in Nashville and Middle Tennessee went if they wanted to go to a state park.

All that was about to change. The ugly thread of segregation, both law and custom in the South for decades, was about to be challenged by the stronger thread of civil rights. The South and the nation would never be the same!

Segregation Out!

Besides the Cold War, the 1950s and '60s brought another challenge for Paris and the South as well: civil rights. This really hit home! One day in May, 1954, the *Nashville Banner* arrived as usual. The headline contained a big word I had never seen before: "SEGREGATION OUT."

I asked my mother what "segregation" meant. I don't remember exactly what she said but I do remember feeling she was very uncomfortable explaining it. I remember how uncomfortable this subject made other grown-ups feel all around me. This discomfort would not go away!

A couple of weeks later, our copy of *LIFE* magazine arrived. This was a special issue called "Background to Segregation." There were full-color illustrations of slavery in all its horror and ugliness: the lower decks of a slave ship, naked men and women in chains, being whipped, and so forth. I was appalled and sickened, yet intrigued as well. They never taught us about this in school!

Our family had a black maid, as did many white, middle-class families. One hot summer day, I rode with Mom as she took the lady home, which was across town in a black neighborhood. On the return trip, I asked my mother why the "colored people" (the term I had been taught was correct) all lived "over there" and we all lived "over here."

There was a long silence. I knew I had asked her another difficult question. Finally, she answered, "Well, Ben, Jr., it's customary." I didn't know what that word meant either and Mom had to explain that, too. In other words, it was yet another Paris and, I later learned—Southern tradition. This all bothered me because I had other questions. I still do!

I never saw any black kids my own age because they all went to their own school, as we white kids did. The only "colored" people I ever actually talked to were maids, cooks, and so forth.

And Dave Travis, who worked at Howard & Jobe. His job title was "porter." He was a part of our family store for many years as long as I can remember.

I have already told you how Dave "chauffeured" my grandpa Horace around town in that 1939 Pontiac. I observed him doing many things for my father and they all seemed to be important. I remember how classy he looked at work, wearing his white linen jacket. So I was totally unprepared for an off-the-cuff remark from a school classmate one day in the early 1960s:

"Ben, is your daddy a nigger lover?!"

I never heard my parents use the N-word. I heard other grown-ups use it more and more as the 1950s moved into the 1960s, and most who said it were angry when they did. So when I heard this fellow at school—-whom I barely knew—ask this question, it made me angry, too. It bothered me that some kid I hardly knew would talk this way about my father.

That evening at home, I asked my father what the kid at school had meant, leaving out the N-word. Dad answered very carefully (the same careful way Mom answered my questions about "segregation" and our maid's housing situation). His answer went something like this: "Well, Ben, I guess he is talking about Dave being head of the local chapter of the NAACP!"

I asked Dad if that was a problem. He said, "No, but I wish Dave wouldn't talk so much on the phone!" That was all. (NAACP stands for the National Association for the Advancement of Colored People.)

I had heard about the NAACP. Some angry whites vowed it was really a Communist-front group. I even heard some (white) adults say Martin Luther King himself was a Communist! I wonder what those same people, if they were still alive today, would think about our nation celebrating MLK Day every January! Or the large granite statue of him unveiled recently in Washington, DC.

When I was twelve or thirteen, I learned about the Holocaust. I am still fascinated with this horrific crime and have found opportunities to teach my students about it as a college speech professor. Adolph Hitler was famously an excellent public speaker!

African-Americans were not the only minority in Paris. There were a few Jews as well, mostly merchants like my family. There were stores with names like Feigenbaum, Weinberg, Greenstone, and Goldstein. My parents bought their first post-war car, a 1947 Buick, from Sam Cohn Buick.

In high school a curious thing happened. Some friend began teasing me about "Howard & Jobe's Jew store!" An issue of my high-school paper carried a list of "Lost and Found" ads. One said: Lost—one skullcap. Return to Ben Jobe!

In 2002, after a lifetime of "Jewish jokes" and getting to know some real Jewish people on my own, I decided to take a DNA genetic test. To my surprise, I found my ancestry is a mixture of English, Irish, Danish, and Eastern European Ashkenazi (derived from the Hebrew word *Ashkenaz* for "German") Jewish!

The Ku Klux Klan and other white-supremacist groups regularly include Jews among the people they hate along with African-Americans. Some of these groups are neo-Nazis so that's no big surprise!

Thus the "Dave Travis" question from my high-school classmate so long ago was one of series of wake-up calls about racism and evil in general I did not have to leave Paris to learn about. Events in my hometown and the larger world outside began these lessons early.

I remember Brother O. E. Turner, the pastor who baptized me at the First Baptist Church, speaking about racism during this period. I don't remember what he was preaching about, but he paused and said: "Folks, racial prejudice is one of the dirtiest, foulest, blackest sins anyone can commit!" He paused dramatically to let the message sink in. The stunned silence was so intense you could almost hear it!

One reason I was genuinely shocked by racism in my sheltered childhood world was because my own immediate family members did not speak of it and went out of their way to treat everyone the same. One might say it was good for business. That's true, but I believe it was also because my family took seriously the command of Jesus: the Golden Rule (Matthew 7:12).

My cousin Bill shared this story with me in a letter not long after I told him about meeting Coach Ben. It seems Grandpa Horace was friends with Dr. Mordecai Johnson, a native of Henry County who was the first African-American president of Howard University. Howard, in Washington, DC, is one of the most noted private historically black universities in America.

This story probably dates from the 1940s. By then, Horace would come by the store for a few hours daily, but left the day-to-day details of the business to his sons, Uncle Howard and Ben, my father. It was summertime and Dr. Johnson came by the store asking about Horace. He was in town to visit family and wanted to see my grandpa as well.

They told him Mr. Horace had been there but had already gone home. Dr. Johnson drove to Horace's place. He went to the side door and knocked. Horace let him in, but asked Dr. Johnson why he had not simply come to the front door!

It was "customary" for a black visitor to a white home to go the side or back door. Washington, DC, and nearby Virginia and Maryland were also segregated during this time. Dr. Johnson was just following "the rules."

Horace and Dr. Johnson continued to keep in touch whenever he came to Paris. I imagine Horace was fascinated by a local man who had become a college president. Paris has not produced that many others, only four I know of. Dr. Johnson was one of two African-Americans among them.

Dave Travis was the store's only black employee but he did not wait on customers unless it was very busy. Even then, he only helped other African-Americans. He would give their money to a white clerk who would make change. The cash register was off limits to him!

Howard & Jobe did not have a black salesperson and, as far as I know, never did. During the mid-1970s, a very bright, attractive young black woman who was a student at a nearby college and a native Parisian, applied for a job as clerk. My parents discussed it thoroughly and then turned her down. I was disappointed but realized they were thinking of the business first. Mom said, "Our customers are simply not ready!"

Ready or not, today it is not unusual for a person of color to wait on a white customer, or vice versa, at least here in Nashville and across much of the South.

As a high-school student, in the summers I worked for the store until my senior year. One bright morning in the summer of 1962, I believe it was, Dad sent me to the Commercial Bank (where he was a director!) to get change for the day's business.

There was a row of ancient wooden benches that ringed the square on all four sides. Each one had in large white capital letters the words WHITE or COLORED, depending on the bench. The letters were so large you could not miss them!

On this sunny summer morning, I suddenly noticed all the benches had a fresh coat of dark green paint. The words WHITE and COLORED had literally disappeared! Such were the "signs" of social change as it moved slowly across Paris and the rest of the South.

That fall, local schools began some token desegregation. A few black students who applied were accepted to attend white schools. My cousin Bill told me one of the first to be accepted was Wilson Kendall, who was the same age as my sister Marilyn. Wilson was one of the few black kids I knew a little because his mother,

Dora, was the maid for Howard & Jobe and also for Uncle Howard's household.

My sister remembered Wilson very well. They were in the same seventh-grade homeroom. She said he was very popular because he was funny. She called him a "cutup." There were a few black students in the ninth grade in the 1962–-63 school year, and even fewer in higher grades.

Black students in Paris formerly attended Henry County Training School for primary grades and then Central High School. When city schools were desegregated in the 1960s, these all-black schools closed. In 1969, a new consolidated Henry County High School replaced all the other high schools, including Grove, which became a junior high.

The prospect of going to school with blacks did not sit well with some of my white classmates. I remember a couple of boys bragging they were going to "drive down to black bottom and throw a brick" at someone.

Our town did not experience any violence that I know of, but the air was full of fear and hatred for quite a while, and we were supposed to be learning how to be grown-ups! Many of the (white) adults and their kids proved to be terrible role models! But somehow we all lived through it. And, I pray, got over it!

The entire civil-rights era in Paris was filled with surprises—-most of them unpleasant. A number of persons, young and old, whom I had believed to be "nice," turned out to be mean. Many of these attended church and probably considered themselves Christians! This bothered me immensely. It still does!

The civil-rights era in Paris, in a negative way, taught me to relate positively to persons from varied backgrounds. My current career as an adjunct professor at Nashville-area public colleges requires me to do this daily. Living through the end of the Jim Crow era turned out to be a blessing, but at the time it was happening, it probably seemed like a curse to some!

I will close with a brief story my mother told me that probably happened about 1965 or '66. And a final observation about how my hometown has progressed down this path more recently.

It was fall of 1965 or '66, because Mom (and sometimes Dad, too) would faithfully attend home football games of Grove High School to hear my sister Marilyn play in the band. (She graduated in 1967; I was in Nashville in college.) One Friday night, Mom arrived late and sat in the "visitors" section behind two men.

She listened to their conversation, which went something like this:

"I think ours is faster than theirs."

"No, man, didn't you see that?! Theirs just outran ours, so you owe me some money!"

Mom believed the two men had bet on which team's black player was the fastest! At least it was a friendly good-natured argument.

During this time, my mother became a Sidney Poitier fan. She left me her own VHS tape of his Oscar-winning film (Best Actor) *"Lilies of the Field."* When some of Poitier's other films came out, like *"Guess Who's Coming to Dinner"* and *"In the Heat of the Night"* (on which the television series was based), she made a point of letting me know about them. I remember seeing *"In the Heat of the Night"* in Nashville.

Millions of white Americans loved this pioneering black actor, with good reason. I am still a fan of Poitier, but also like Morgan Freeman, Denzel Washington, and Cuba Gooding, Jr., to name a few more personal favorites.

Fast-forward to 1996: Tennessee's Bicentennial, celebrating two hundred years of the Volunteer State's history. Paris is almost as old as the state. It was founded in 1823 and named in honor of the French patriot Lafayette who was visiting the United States at the time.

By the 1990s, a black man, Samuel D. Tharpe, was vice-mayor! He was elected mayor in 2008 and was reelected in 2012. This is even more remarkable when you consider that historically only about 20 percent, one in five Parisians, have been African-American. Paris is in step with the rest of the nation in this important area. I'm proud of my hometown!

Part Three:

Family Fabric

"Honor your father and your mother, that your days may be prolonged in the land which the Lord your God gives you"

(Exodus 20:12).

The thread of my father's life began on October 19, 1906. Ben Anderson Jobe, Sr., was born at home as was his older brother, Howard, had been five years earlier. Home was a modest four-room frame dwelling on Head Street, about a mile from downtown.

The house did not have central heat. A single fireplace heated all four rooms. The house may have had running water but probably no indoor plumbing. As of 1910, only about one in seven American homes had a bathtub!

My cousin Bill says his father, Howard, adored his younger brother, Ben, five years his junior. The boys grew and by the time he was twelve, Howard was considered old enough by Grandpa Horace to be sent by train to St. Louis on a buying trip—alone!

Ben attended the first three grades across town at Robert E. Lee Elementary School. In 1915, a new school opened much closer to their home: Atkins-Porter. Dad attended fourth through eighth grades there.

I am sure he worked at Howard & Jobe early on. It was expected he and his older brother would follow in their father's footsteps and someday inherit the business.

He also held at least one other job I know of. Dad told me when he was twelve or thirteen, he worked after school and during the summer for a drugstore on the square near Howard & Jobe. He made deliveries on his bicycle.

When he was not making deliveries, Dad said he was required to be in the back of the store, bottling a special patent medicine: "for man and beast"" the label said. There was a large barrel containing this magical elixir. My father was to fill, label, and seal as many bottles as he could between deliveries!

The family was active in the First Baptist Church, only a block off the courthouse square. When he was twelve, my father made a profession of faith in Christ and was baptized. As a teenager, he was active in the "young people's union," which met on Sunday evenings.

Ben attended Grove High School from 1920 through his graduation in 1924. He was named "most popular boy" as a senior—an honor that he shared in a tie vote with his lifelong friend Robert Arnett. My father was also trainer for the football team, the Grove Blue Devils. I am sure he worked for Howard & Jobe off and on all through high school.

In the fall of 1924, Dad became the first in our family to attend college: the University of Tennessee in Knoxville. He double majored in business and finance. He was also a member of Sigma Chi fraternity.

To get to and from UT, Dad took the train. There was no direct route. He rode the L & N north to Bowling Green, Kentucky, then south to Nashville and the Nashville, Chattanooga, and St. Louis line southeast to Chattanooga. From there, he took another rail line northeast to Knoxville. The trip consumed most of a day or night. Today, you can drive south from Paris on US Highway 641 to Interstate 40, and take the interstate all the way to Knoxville in much less time.

The University of Tennessee in Knoxville was much smaller then. Dad said it had fewer than two thousand students in the 1920s. Today, UT's total enrollment is around thirty thousand! My adult son Joshua, a certified public accountant in Atlanta, has bachelor's and master's degrees from UT.

Just before Dad was to begin his final quarter as a senior, he suffered an attack of appendicitis while in Paris.

At this time, the town had only a couple of clinics, not a full-fledged hospital. He was rushed to Nashville's St. Thomas Hospital where an appendectomy was performed. He recovered from the surgery at home.

However, when he was well, Horace forbade him to return to UT and finish! Not being allowed to complete his degree and graduate after years of hard work really hurt my dad!

Horace apparently saw it differently. He had paid good money for his son's education. His son had been away nearly four years and that was long enough! Horace was impatient to get a return on his investment.

My father mentioned this from time to time when I was in college in the 1960s. He urged me to stay in school and graduate. He did not have to insist too much, as by then the Vietnam War and my student draft deferment made other equally- convincing arguments!

So in 1928, my father returned to the family business. The next year, the stock market crashed on Wall Street. In time, its ripple effects began to impact Tennessee and Paris with it. The order of the day for most Americans was simply to survive. By the grace of God, my father and Howard & Jobe did.

However, the Depression years offered some bright spots. In the summer of 1931, Dad and his high-school friend Robert Arnett embarked on a "grand tour" of Europe. They were gone for six weeks, stopping in England, France, Italy, Switzerland, and Germany.

In Berlin, Dad recalled hearing the sound of glass breaking in the quiet of the night. The next morning, across the street from his hotel, the windows of a store had been smashed. In large black letters, vandals had painted the word "JUDE"—-JEW! This was in summer, 1931, about a year and a half before Adolph Hitler and the Nazi Party came to power. But this deed had Nazi fingerprints all over it.

Dad told me stories like this as I grew up. His European trip was like getting a college degree and perhaps compensated a little for not being allowed to graduate from UT.

Two other bright spots were his niece Jean and nephew Bill, who were born in 1927 and '28, respectively. During the Depression years when they were growing up, they spent much time with "Uncle B" who loved them like his own children.

Cousin Bill recalls spending the night with "Uncle B" often in the drafty old frame house on Head Street. By 1940, Horace believed the worst of the Depression was over and bought a larger brick home on Jackson Street, one block closer to downtown. He and Inez lived there until their deaths in 1953 and 1951, respectively.

My father had some girlfriends during the Depression years, but economic uncertainties must have made him think twice about getting married. That was typical of the period. The Depression caused many Americans to put their plans on hold, sometimes for years.

During the '30s, my father lived at home, like many other single adults in America, and saved his money. At some point, he had an opportunity to buy a few shares of stock in the Commercial Bank & Trust Company, where Howard & Jobe did business.

This proved to be a smart move. When he and my mother became sole owners of the store in 1961, Dad's seat on the board of directors of the bank, Henry County''s oldest and largest at the time, was a valuable financial resource for both Howard & Jobe and our family as well.

My father told me his grandfather, Ben Avant Jobe, besides being a gentleman farmer in northern Henry County after the Civil War, was also on the board of directors of a bank in Puryear for many years. As a sideline, he made loans to men he knew personally who had been turned down for a loan by the bank!

My great-grandfather would loan money only to men he knew to be reliable and trustworthy. Even so, not all of these men could get a bank loan. I wonder if Great-Grandpa ever had someone default on a loan. I like to think his Civil War experiences helped him to be a good judge of character.

By 1940, my father had saved around ten thousand dollars! He was thirty-three years old in March that year and considered by some to be the town's most eligible bachelor. So it was no surprise when his pastor, Hansel Stembridge of First Baptist Church, asked him to meet a young female guest whom the pastor had invited to

Paris to speak to the church's young people. He had heard her speak earlier at the Tennessee Baptist Convention's annual meeting in Chattanooga.

The young woman was Mary Alice Hall, twenty-one, from Mt. Pleasant in Maury County. A petite brunette, she stood only four feet, eleven inches! But her dynamic personality and public-speaking skills had so impressed Pastor Stembridge at the state meeting, he wanted the youth of his church in Paris to hear her.

I believe he also had another agenda—matchmaker for Paris's most eligible bachelor! He introduced my parents literally on the front steps of the church and asked my father to show the attractive young woman around town.

Mom was a senior at Tennessee College for Women in Murfreesboro. It was the only Baptist all-female four-year college in the state. Founded in 1906, the year my father was born, TCW promptly closed in 1946 following the end of World War II. After all, what young woman in her right mind would go to an all-female school in 1946 when all those GI's were back home?!

Mary Alice Hall spoke to the young people on a Friday evening. Then there was a meal. They seated her between my father and another man who was superintendent of the Paris City schools.

Mom had gone to college to become a teacher. She said at the church supper the one man she most wanted to talk to was not my father. It was the other man who was superintendent of the Paris City schools. She was graduating in June and needed a job!

Mother did not have to worry. She was hired by Murfreesboro's Central High School to teach English and speech upon her graduation. She signed a contract for the 1940–41 school year.

But the young man sitting on her other side at the church supper that night was undaunted. He asked her out. In fact, when word got around Paris of the pretty young woman visiting from out of town, there were a number of other interested young men. My father had the advantage, thanks to his pastor.

After Mom returned to college in Murfreesboro to complete her degree, Dad began a long-distance courtship, which included frequent Sunday trips to and from the Middle Tennessee town. Driving from Paris to Murfreesboro in 1940 took several hours. Dad would try to arrive there in time to take her to lunch. They would spend most of the afternoon together, then Dad would begin the long drive back home.

In June, following her graduation, Mom accepted Dad's invitation to spend a weekend at the summer home of some friends of his near Savannah, Tennessee. On a warm summer evening, while sitting on their screened-in porch watching the sun set over the Tennessee River, my father proposed to my mother.

She accepted, but asked to be allowed to fulfill her contract to teach the one year in Murfreesboro. When she told me this story, Mom said she did not realize the school authorities would probably have released her from her contract for a reason like marriage!

After a long year of waiting, the wedding finally took place at First Baptist Church in Mt. Pleasant on September 7, 1941. Pastor Stembridge performed the ceremony. He missed a turn somewhere on the way between Paris and Mt. Pleasant and arrived late. But Ben and Mary finally became husband and wife. The threads of their lives were finally woven together in a distinctive pattern.

The newlyweds honeymooned in New York City. Dad drove Mom to Washington, DC, where they caught a train. Their stay in Manhattan included fine restaurants and a couple of Broadway shows. After a week in the Big Apple, they returned to Paris to begin their new life together.

Even though Dad had saved several thousand dollars and could afford it, he and Mom decided not to buy a house. They lived with Horace and Inez in their brick house on Jackson Street.

This proved to be a wise decision. Three months to the day after they were married, on December 7, 1941, Pearl Harbor was bombed by the Japanese. For the United States, a long four-year struggle began that would change Paris, the state, the nation, and world: World War II. This global conflict would leave nations, families and individuals with threads of triumph and tragedy, victory and defeat, rejoicing and mourning.

Part Three: Family Fabric

Top Left/Right: Uncle Howard, 23, *left* and My Dad, 17, *right* (1924)/ My Mom Mary Hall, cheerleader, *front row center* (1935).

Center Left/Right: My Mother at age 21(1940)/ Howard & Jobe store, before remodel (late 1940s).

Bottom: My parents' wedding, First Baptist Church, Mt. Pleasant, TN. (September 7th 1941).

Common Threads

Top: Howard & Jobe interior before remodel (late1940s)

Center Left/Middle/Right: My Father in his army uniform(1943)/ My Grandfather Horace E. Jobe, at age 83, at the store's 50th anniversary (1951)/ Store after remodel (1951)

Bottom Left/Right: My Fifth Birthday Party, at Joyland Kindergarten, Paris, TN, *I'm wearing a crown, on the back row right*(10-17-1950)/ My First Grade Christmas Program, at Atkins-Porter Elementary School, *I'm in the front row center*(12-20-1951)

Part Three: Family Fabric

Top Left/Right: Flower Girls: Susan Cecil and my sister Marilyn (*right*)(6-26-1953)/ My Sister Marilyn's Sixth Birthday Party, Paris, *TN,she and I are wearing crowns(* 6-20-1955)

Middle Left/Right: God & Country Award Ceremony, Boy Scout Troop 23, *I am second from the right*(3-15-1959)/ Grove High School Speech Trip, to Muskogee, OK, *I am front row extreme right , Ruby and Clem Krider are in the center*(11-19-1959)

Bottom Left/Right: "Mr. Cool" at school! Graduation from Murray State University, KY, (August 1976)/ My Son Joshua, at age 8, Franklin, TN (1988)

Photos from Tom Lonardo of Memphis, TN.

His father was a professional musician who had a swing band and a music store where I bought much piano music while growing up. The Lonardos lived across the street from us. Tom Lonardo, Sr., came from Rhode Island to serve @ an Army camp outside Paris during WWII, married a local lady and stayed the rest of his life!

Mom's Family:

Grays, Halls, Durhams, and Hurds

I have told you about family threads of the Jobes of Paris and Henry County.

Now it's the turn of my mom's family.

We are primarily concerned here with my maternal grandmother Ada Bryan Gray's parents, George Washington Gray and his Texas wife Mary Womack Gray. He had met her in Dallas while attending the Southern Baptist Convention. (When I was a toddler just learning to talk, I mispronounced my grandmother's name Ada as "Deda." The nickname stuck.)

Deda's parents lived in Summertown, Tennessee (Lawrence County), where "Papa" Gray was its first mayor. His wife Mary was the town's only telephone operator for several years. The telephone exchange was in their home but I doubt if there were many calls in the middle of the night.

George and Mary Gray were the parents of five children: Sam, Winnie, Elmo, Ada and Mary Gracie, an infant who died with her mother in childbirth. Ada (aka "Deda") was born on December 17, 1896. Her father gave her the middle name Bryan after the famous politician William Jennings Bryan. She was four when her mother died.

Papa Gray did not wait long to remarry after his wife died. He married Marcella Pugh, from Lawrence County, Tennessee and they never had any children. My mother always had the impression Marcella Pugh (who was called "Granny") was not too keen on rearing a four-year-old. The other children, being older, were soon grown and gone from home.

Presumably by mutual agreement, Papa Gray and his sister Ada decided "little Ada" should be reared by her aunt Ada and her husband, Walter N. Durham. The Durhams operated a grocery store in Summertown and had no children of their own.

It seemed to be an ideal arrangement. Uncle Newt Durham was also a lay preacher but never pastored a church. Deda always said they were very good to her but strict and not openly affectionate. Perhaps that explains why Mom recalled few hugs as she grew up. Deda was not demonstrative because she herself had received few hugs.

The Grays also operated a grocery store in Summertown but soon after Papa Gray's second marriage, he and "Granny" moved to Ridley, about two miles north of Mt. Pleasant, where he owned and operated a large, old-fashioned general store with his home right next door.

Eventually, the Durhams also moved to Mt. Pleasant from Summertown and owned and operated a grocery store on Locust Street right next door to their house. This is where Mom lived from the time her father, John Harvey Hall, died when Mom was fourteen months old until Deda married "Bandaddy" (my nickname for Mr. Hurd) when Mom was six.

We have a couple of old photos of John Harvey Hall. I look a lot like him!

However, Mom never knew him because she was an infant when he died.

When Mom was in the first grade, the first signature on her report card was "Mrs. Ada Hall" and the rest were "Mrs. Ada Hurd"! For years Mom referred to 1926 as "when we married Mr. Hurd!"!

Charles Franklin Hurd, who I called "Bandaddy," was born on February 17, 1875, and died on May 12, 1955. At the time of his marriage to Ada Gray Hall on January 18, 1926, he was fifty, had been married before and had three daughters by his first wife. He was an engineer for the Louisville & Nashville Railroad and an Episcopalian.

Mammy and Uncle Newt may been strict and not openly affectionate with Deda, but twice in her life they gave her a home when she had nowhere else to go: when she was motherless at the age of four and when she was widowed with a sickly child at age twenty-three. Mom was always grateful to both of them.

In fact, the Durhams seemed more like grandparents to my mother than Papa Gray. She adored them, especially Uncle Newt who spoiled her ridiculously. She was his only "grandchild" and he was her surrogate grandfather. Mom never knew her other three grandparents, as they all died before she was born.

Mom never knew how her mother and father met. John Harvey Hall was originally from Huntsville, Alabama, and twelve years older than Deda. He was the chief bookkeeper for the Charleston Mining Company, Arrow Mine branch, just a mile or so outside Mt. Pleasant. (Maury County was well known for its phosphate mining.,)

When they were first married, my mother's parents lived in a small "company house" at Arrow Mines where Mom was born. Deda always said that little house was so cold!

Mom also did not know until she was a grown woman her father had a brief, childless marriage to a woman named Mabel sometime before he met Deda. That marriage had ended in divorce before he met Deda.

John Harvey Hall and Ada Bryan Gray were married on September 16, 1917. Their only child, my mother, was born on December 30, 1918. The little family soon moved to Mt. Pleasant to a small, white frame "rental" house on North Main Street.

The marriage was cut short when my grandfather died of flu and pneumonia (just a few years before penicillin was invented) on February 20, 1920. He had been born on January 12, 1885, which made him just thirty-five.

Deda was only twenty-three, had no marketable skills, and had only completed the ninth grade. It was a time of unspeakable desolation for her. Mom was not a healthy child, having chronic colitis as a baby and having learned to walk a second time.

My grandmother did the best she could under the circumstances. She and her infant daughter went back to live with Mammy and Uncle Newt. She also got a job clerking in a Jewish-owned department store, Stein's in downtown Mt. Pleasant.

There were no daycare centers in those days so Mom spent her first six months under Mammy's watch care. She said her cousin Helen Wilson was her only playmate and friend.

Though Mammy and Uncle Newt never formally adopted Deda, they did give her (and Mom once) a home and we're glad Deda was able in a sense to pay them back later. No one knew Mammy had heart trouble. Uncle Newt kept his grocery open late every night. It was a kind of "gathering place" for the neighborhood.

One night he went to the house where they lived next door to the grocery and ate his supper. Mammy seemed fine. Two hours later when he closed the grocery and went home, she was sitting peacefully in her favorite rocking chair—quite dead. It was a great shock and grief to the whole family.

Deda was married to Mr. Hurd by this time and he, she and Mom moved in with Uncle Newt. Deda gave him a good home, good meals and companionship for the rest of his life, so the debt was partially paid.

You may be wondering why Uncle Newt did not leave his house to Deda. He should have. However, in spite of many endearing qualities, he was not a good businessman. He never would press people about what they owed.

When he died, all of his property including the grocery, his home, and five rental houses he had built were mortgaged to the hilt. After the sale of his property and payment of all the debts, there was nothing left.

Mom was always grateful she was born and raised in a Christian atmosphere. Her family members were not articulate believers, but they were *faithful*. A Bible verse says, "A good name is rather to be chosen than great riches" (Proverbs 22:1).

Mom's earliest memories were of sitting on a hard wooden pew in the little white frame First Baptist Church in Mt. Pleasant with her feet dangling over the edge quite a distance from the floor.

Deda had been a church pianist when she was sixteen. My mother inherited her musical gifts from her and passed them on to me and my sister. The upright piano in our Paris home had originally belonged to Deda. I used to make noises (not music!) on it as a child when we visited her in Mt. Pleasant.

Mom attended school in Mt. Pleasant. She was so advanced academically, they allowed her to skip the second grade! Mom later said this had been a mistake, as it made her always the youngest in her class.

At Haylong High School, she was a cheerleader all four years. During her senior year, she was the only girl on the squad! She was also an active member of First Baptist Church, especially in music. I believe she also taught a Sunday School class, something Mom would do most of her life!

From there, she became the first in her family—like my father—to go to college—Tennessee College for Women in Murfreesboro. Her activities included being class president her first two years, dean's list, various musical and dramatic organizations, and the yearbook staff. She was also head of the archery team one year! As a senior, Mom was named to Who's Who Among Students in American Universities and Colleges.

She also dated a young man for over two years who was going to be a preacher. He was convinced it was God's will they marry. Mom was not convinced. They eventually went their separate ways. By the time she and my father met early in 1940, Mom was single. All that remained was for her to meet my Dad. By September 7, 1941, the threads of their lives had been woven together in a new pattern.

Newlyweds in Wartime

A few months after Pearl Harbor was attacked and the United State declared war, Dad was drafted. Mom saw him off on the train, then went into the depot— ladies' restroom and cried!

This may have been providential, but the effects of a childhood illness kept Dad from being sent overseas. He was fairly healthy as a child, except for a case of rheumatic fever in the fourth grade. It left him with an irregular heartbeat: a heart "murmur."

When Dad reported for his physical, he told the military doctor about his heart murmur. The doctor examined him thoroughly and wrote something on Dad's chart. Then he stepped out of the room. Dad took advantage of being alone to read what the doctor had written: "Soldier says he has heart murmur but I hear none."

Despite his doctor's doubts, Dad was not sent overseas. Instead, he was assigned to Camp Wolters in Mineral Wells, Texas, west of Fort Worth. After a few months, Mom joined him there.

Dad was given a job supervising German prisoners-of- war who worked repairing uniforms, duffel bags, and other war-related materiel. He worked the graveyard shift, 11:00 p.m. to 7:00 a.m., for two- and- a- half years.

When I was about ten, Dad gave me a little booklet the army had given him called *Getting Along in German*. It was a primer for the beginning German speaker!— I remember walking around our house in Paris counting out loud from one to twenty in German. I'm sure I made a nuisance of myself!

Dad's wartime job with those German POWs planted the seeds of my lifelong fascination with Hitler and the Holocaust. This has helped me teach speech to my college classes today.

His work had its points of interest. Some of the Germans spoke English. One man, who had been an actor before the war, told Dad, "When *we* win the war, I'm going to Hollywood!" The power of Nazi propaganda!

He and Mom rented an apartment. She got a secretarial job in the office of a local Baptist church. Mom told me several times this is when their marriage really took off. They were finally on their own, in their own home. It had been a long wait.

From time to time, family members came to visit. Since Deda was married to a Louisville & Nashville Railroad engineer, she had a pass that allowed her to travel on any rail line in the country. She came out to Texas more than once to see her daughter and son-in-law. Bill and Jean came, too, to see "Uncle B" and their new "Aunt Mary."

It was during a summer visit to see "Uncle B" and "Aunt Mary" when my cousins Jean and Bill became enamored with Texas, and especially Baylor University. Mom taught the girls' high-school Sunday school class at the church where she also worked. Dad taught the boys' class. (He did this after working all the previous night at the army base!)

Bill and Jean both met youth their own age with some connection to Baylor—either they were planning to go there or had an older sibling who already did. They both talked about how friendly these Texas young people were! That's how my cousins ended up attending college in Texas after the war. And probably why my cousin Bill has lived in the Lone Star State since 1960.

Peacetime Baby Boom

My parents were finally on their own and very much in love. Confident in the ultimate Allied victory, they began trying to start a family. After praying one day, Mom said she was overwhelmed by the presence of the Lord. Not long afterward, she visited her doctor and he gave her the good news: she was pregnant. The thread of my life had begun!

I was nearly born in Texas. Mineral Wells did not have the medical facilities Fort Worth did. So my parents were planning to have me delivered in a Fort Worth hospital in late September, 1945.

But the war ended before that could happen. Following the dropping of atomic bombs on Hiroshima and Nagasaki in August, the Japanese surrendered a short time later. By September, my parents were on their way back home to Tennessee. Dad took a train from

Paris to Atlanta to be discharged from the army at Fort McPherson.

Like millions of other servicemen, he became a veteran. Many did not return. Many more returned with inward and outward scars of war that changed them forever. I am grateful to all the men and women who safeguarded and preserved our freedom during that global conflict. I still have the greatest appreciation for all who serve our country in the military today.

My soon-to-be parents rented a modest apartment in a house on Dunlap Street, a few blocks from downtown and Howard & Jobe. Dad returned to work for the family business. Mom got ready for motherhood.

I was born on October 17, at Nobles Memorial Hospital, a two-story brick building a few blocks west of downtown. Mom said her labor lasted nearly twenty-four hours! She and Dad, typical of their generation, had been born at home. My sister and I, like millions of other post-war baby boomers, were born in a hospital.

In 1946, our family moved from the apartment on Dunlap Street to a two-bedroom, one-bath brick home Dad had purchased at 315 Jackson Street. The house had a fireplace in the living room. It also had a basement with a coal-burning furnace that heated the entire house.

Later, they had an attic fan installed in the ceiling of the main hallway, to cool us on hot summer nights. Homes were not air-conditioned yet. A few businesses were, like our store beginning in 1947. The Capitol and Princess Theaters had been the first in town with air-conditioning.

It was about this same time they bought a new Buick from Sam Cohn, the local Buick dealer. It was a black, two-door sedan. There was a huge pent-up demand for new cars, as none had been manufactured during the war.

I remember taking a trip with my parents to Gulfport, Mississippi, in the summer of 1948 in our Buick. The sand on the beach was so white it shimmered! I remember how tingly the salt water felt as it touched my toes.

Mom explained we were in "Mississippi."

"Where is Mister Sippy?" I asked.

In the fall of 1948, I was told that next year, I would have either a baby brother or sister. Having been the center of attention all my life, I was not thrilled by this news. I said, "You don't want a baby!"— mixing up my pronouns.

My sister, Marilyn Hall Jobe, was born June 20, 1949, also at Nobles Hospital. Our family was now complete. Once Marilyn was born, I changed my tune. I liked having a baby sister.

The fall of 1950 was time for kindergarten. My parents sent me to a privately owned place called Joyland. Our teacher was a Mrs. Dinkins. She made kindergarten lots of fun. All the kids were given a birthday party. When my fifth birthday came in October, I had one as well.

In 1954–55, Marilyn also attended Joyland. Her sixth birthday party was held in the side yard of our new home at 508 Jackson Street on June 20th, 1955.

The winter of 1950–51 was bitterly cold with lots of snow. Mom took a picture of me standing outside the front of Howard & Jobe next to a large pile of snow and ice that had been shoveled to make way for traffic. I remember playing in the snow, all bundled up.

In the late 1940s, my parents had built a two-story red brick duplex in the lot next to our home on Jackson Street. They became landlords. One of their earliest renters was a family from Michigan named Hoffmeister. They had two young children. Mr. Hoffmeister worked for the Holley Carburetor plant that had just opened. Holley was a Michigan company so they sent many people to the Paris plant over the years.

Even after they moved to the new house at 508 Jackson, my parents kept the duplex. They eventually sold it to a tenant in the late 1950s.

In the fall of 1951, I began the first grade at Atkins-Porter Elementary School where my father had also attended. I remember being in the Christmas play. Christmas plays and similar events have largely disappeared from public schools now because of "political correctness."

My grandmother Inez died on March 5, 1951, at the age of seventy-six. Grandma Inez was a loving, rather quiet woman. My father's temperament was closer to hers than to Horace's. I remember her funeral. It was a cold rainy day as we stood beside her grave at Maplewood Cemetery. This was the first funeral of a family member I can recall—my first experience with death.

Grandpa Horace had married Inez on April 26, 1900. They were together over half a century. After Inez died, his health began to fail. Horace developed leukemia and died on November 5, 1953. He was eighty-five.

Grandpa Horace and Inez had lived at 318 Jackson Street since about 1940. This was not far from our first home at 315. I remember walking with Dad many evenings after supper from 315 to 318 Jackson to visit them. Dad would carry my baby sister, Marilyn, on his shoulders.

Grandpa had a big cabinet radio in the living room. We would listen to *"The Lone Ranger."* I remember its rhythmic theme music, which, years later, I learned was a famous classical piece called *"William Tell Overture."* This is probably my earliest memory of music besides what we heard at church.

I remember my Grandpa cutting up an apple and giving us each a slice. Grandma Inez would say, in her soft voice, "Now, Horace, be careful and don't cut yourself!" He would ignore her and go right on cutting. But she had done her duty and warned him. I never saw him slice himself instead of the apple.

My Paris family was not the only thread in my life. There was my Middle Tennessee grandma, whose life was bound even more tightly to mine.

Middle Tennessee Grandma

I was not as close to my Jobe grandparents as I was to Deda. Grandma Inez Jobe had died when I was just five-and-a-half; Grandpa Horace left us when I was only eight. There was another reason Deda and I were very close—I apparently looked a lot like my maternal grandfather John Harvey Hall. But I did not learn this until I was almost eighteen.

Shortly after World War II ended, Mr. Hurd—who I called "Bandaddy"—retired from his long career as a Louisville & Nashville Railroad engineer. He had diabetes. About 1948, he underwent surgery to remove one leg just above the knee. He also required daily shots of insulin, which Deda administered faithfully.

I visited them whenever I could, especially in summer. Their Mt. Pleasant home had a large backyard with a chicken coop, an outhouse left over from an earlier era (they now had indoor plumbing) and a storm cellar.

This was kept locked at all times, which just pricked my curiosity. Once or twice, I persuaded Deda to open it so I could peer inside. The storm cellar was dark, smelly, and nasty. Once or twice was enough!

On my summer visits during the 1950s, she would sometimes send me to gather the eggs. This was a novelty since I was not a farm kid. At some point, the chicken coop was empty. But I had enjoyed the live chickens and fresh homegrown eggs while the coop was full. Good food was part of the Deda experience. She was the best cook I knew—Mom included!

The old house on Florida Avenue had a large front porch with a swing. I loved spending time at Deda's place. Besides, they were only fifty miles from Nashville, less than half the distance we were in Paris. Their television signal was much stronger and the picture brighter and sharper than ours in Paris. (This was long before cable. Homes had an outside antenna.)

Early in 1955, Bandaddy developed an infection in his good leg. The infection turned to gangrene. His doctors ruled out surgery because he was eighty years old! He died on May 12, 1955, at the age of eighty years and three months. I remember the funeral in Mt. Pleasant.

Deda lived in their house on Florida Avenue for a few more years, but became increasingly unable to live on her own. My parents persuaded her to sell the house and move to Paris, which she did in 1960. After living with us a few months, she purchased a small duplex in the block north of First Baptist Church. She could walk to church from there. She rented out one side and lived in the other.

Deda lived there until her health failed around Christmas, 1976. Mom put her in a nursing home in Puryear, where she lived another three months. She died on March 17, 1977. She was exactly eighty years and three months old—within a few days of the same age Mr. Hurd had been when he died.

There were two funerals: one in Paris and another the next day in Mt. Pleasant where she was buried. Even though she had been gone from there for seventeen years, a lot of people came by and told how much her life had meant to theirs. This made a powerful impression on me. To me she was Deda, my favorite grandparent. To many of her friends and former neighbors, she was apparently just as special as she was to me. The thread of her life had touched a wide circle of people.

No Place Like Home

The year 1952 was dominated by the construction of our new home—a large three-bedroom, two-bath, one-story red brick structure at 508 Jackson Street. I remember going with my parents and sister many times to see how it was progressing. It was much bigger than our older home at 315 Jackson.

Mom and Dad had purchased two lots, side by side, on the corner of Jackson and Highland Streets. Atkins-Porter School was on Walnut Street, one block north, within easy walking distance. Next door to our new home was the backyard of a large home that faced Walnut, across from the school.

The owners, the Mandels, had a large concrete swimming pool! There was a diving board and even a bathhouse. My sister and I were amazed and envious. Mom told us we could not swim there unless we were "invited." In the summer of 1953, we received an invitation.

We enjoyed many cool swims on hot summer days with other select Paris kids. You might have called us the "swimming elite."

I did not know it at the time, but being able to swim anywhere in Paris was something special. There were no swimming pools in any public parks. Access to swimming was limited to Paris Landing State Park, sixteen miles away. Until the Civil Rights Act of 1964 was enacted, state parks in Tennessee and throughout the South were segregated.

In fact, during the 1960s I frequently heard the excuse why no public park in Paris had a pool: the "N— will want to come swim in it!" The Civil Rights Act of 1964 with its public-accommodations section, rendered such arguments mute. Now at least one Paris public park has a swimming pool—for all to enjoy.

On Christmas Eve, 1952, we finally moved into our new home. I remember my sister and I running down the hall on Christmas morning to the den to see what "Santa" had brought. The floors did not have carpeting yet. Large pieces of cardboard served as temporary carpet. The living and dining rooms were likewise not ready and were off limits.

That was the Christmas I got my first bicycle. I also remember getting a few skinned knees learning to ride it. There was not much traffic on our street. On Walnut, one block over, things got busy around A-P School in the mornings and afternoons. As I grew older, I explored farther and farther from home on my bike, often riding downtown to the store, about a mile away.

Our home was one of the largest and finest in the immediate neighborhood, except for the Mandel house whose swimming pool adjoined our side yard. Sidney Mandel—who owned a clay-mining company in the county—had come from St. Louis. Mandel was Jewish. His family was considered to be one of the richest in town.

The corner lot on Jackson at Blanton—--across from the Mandel pool—--had a fine home owned by a Mrs. Bell. It also had a large yard with steep banks. I remember mowing that yard when I was about twelve or thirteen, struggling to keep our family power mower steady on those banks! I earned extra money in summers by mowing neighbors' yards, like many boys my age.

In the spring of 1953, Mom and Dad had the large front and side yards landscaped. As I grew older, it became my job to mow it. I was less impressed with its size then compared to when I was seven or eight years old.

My parents had bought the extra lot, they said, so we kids would have a place to play! Play we did, and other kids in the neighborhood frequently joined us. I remember building several "forts" and "apartments" with leftover bricks, which stayed around for years until I outgrew this particular obsession. I also built a treehouse in the mulberry tree beside my sister's bedroom.

I drove nails directly into its limbs, which took its toll on the tree!

As I grew older, I began to notice how active my parents were in church.

Dad was a deacon. Whenever we observed the Lord's Supper—communion—he was one of the men who passed out the unleavened bread and grape juice. One of my fondest memories of Mom is of her sitting in a large easy chair in their bedroom on Saturday afternoon studying the lesson she would teach in Sunday School the next morning.

In 1954, I met God. I remember having a dream—not once but three times—in which I heard a gentle, loving Voice calling my name. I told my mother. After the third such dream, she took me to visit our pastor, Brother O. E. Turner. He talked with me and asked me a few questions. I finally realized Who the Voice was and answered His call.

The following Sunday, I walked down the aisle at the conclusion of the morning worship service and made a profession of faith in Christ. I was voted into the membership of First Baptist Church, They gave me a Bible with my name and the date written in the front: September 26, 1954. I still have that Bible.

I remember being baptized a few weeks later. By then it was fall, and the water in the baptistery was chilly! But getting baptized was the right thing to do. I had learned in Sunday School how Jesus was nailed to a cross for my sins. I could get a little cold and wet for Him in the baptistery for a few minutes!

My sister, Marilyn, says she wanted to follow in my footsteps when she was six, the next year: 1955. However, Mom and Bro. Turner talked with her and decided she was not "ready." Two more years passed. When Marilyn was eight, in 1957, she took this important step on her own and was baptized.

When I was in the third grade (1953), I joined the Cub Scouts. Marilyn would become a Brownie and later a Girl Scout. The Girl Scout Council had their regional camp on Kentucky Lake near Paris Landing—Camp Hazelwood. Marilyn attended that camp for several summers. She was in Scouting from age seven through fourteen.

When I was eleven, I moved from Cub Scouts to Boy Scouts—Troop 23. The Paris Boy Scouts had their own "Scout house." It was a one-story concrete-block building on a hill overlooking a public-housing project whose residents were poor and black. We met every Monday night so the trip to the Scout house took me right by the housing project.

It never occurred to any of us that our troop and all others in Paris I knew about were all-white. It was only in recent years, while teaching at Tennessee State University in Nashville (our state's only public historically- black school), I have learned about Scout troops for boys of other races!

I dove into Scouting with gusto. We went to summer camp in Benton County, just south of Henry County, at Camp Mack Morris. The camp had rustic cabins and waterfront footage on the Birdsong Creek embayment of Kentucky Lake. I spent a week there each summer for two or three years.

I moved up through the ranks—learning how to camp, hike, swim, and other valuable skills. In 1959, at the age of thirteen, I achieved the highest rank—Eagle, along with several others in our Troop. I earned twenty-four merit badges in my Scouting career.

The highlight of my Scouting experience was the Fiftieth National Jamboree in Colorado Springs in the summer of 1960. We rode a chartered bus from Jackson that left one evening at 7:00 p.m. It was a thirty-six-hour trip across Arkansas, Oklahoma, the Texas Panhandle, and a corner of New Mexico.

We arrived early in the morning in Colorado Springs. I remember chopping yucca bushes to clear our campsite with Pike's Peak standing tall and proud in the distance.

I also remember most of us getting sunburned because the low humidity fooled us into thinking it was not that hot! We were used to humid Tennessee summers, not Colorado's "dry heat." After chopping yucca bushes for several hours, shirtless, most of my friends and I looked like lobsters!

By this time, I was writing for the Grove *Comet*. The *Paris Post-Intelligencer,* called the *P-I,* asked me to be their "press correspondent" for the Jamboree. I had a press pass and special privileges—like getting to attend press conferences.

I especially remember the ones with the lovely Lennon Sisters from the TV show *"Lawrence Welk"* and actor James Arness of *"Gunsmoke"* fame. President Eisenhower also made an appearance at the Jamboree. There were over fifty thousand scouts there, including many from other nations. It was a memorable time in my young life.

I filed my news dispatches—written in longhand—via regular mail, so there was a delay of a few days before they appeared in the Paris paper. It sure makes you appreciate the Internet!

At the conclusion of the Jamboree, Mom, Dad, and Marilyn met me in Colorado Springs and we began a marathon family vacation trip. This was our first such trip west. In 1959, we had spent a week in Washington, DC. The year after, 1961, was the trip to New York. More about that later.

My family drove north from Colorado Springs through Denver to Wyoming. We stopped in Cheyenne. I had a new 35-millimeter camera and lots of film to shoot. I made a point of photographing state capitols: Colorado, Wyoming, South Dakota, and so forth.

We drove north and west through Wyoming to Grand Teton and Yellowstone National Parks. I especially remember a lot of bears and the famous geyser "Old Faithful." From Yellowstone, we turned east and headed home, stopping in the Black Hills of South Dakota to see Mount Rushmore's immense statues of four US presidents.

At Spearfish, South Dakota we saw a "passion play" depicting the last week of Christ's life on earth. I had never seen anything like it. The memory of seeing something I had learned about in church dramatized on the stage stayed with me for a long time.

Many of the actors were a German family who had come to the United States and set up shop in the Black Hills. In 1984, Mom traveled with a tour group to Oberammergau, Germany, to see the 350th season of what was said to be the world's oldest continuous passion play.

From South Dakota, we made our way east and south through Nebraska, Iowa, Missouri, and on home to Paris. I would see some of these same places two years later on the longest speech trip of my life—the National Forensic League national tournament at Montana State University in Missoula.

These family trips were special times for all of us. More than just vacations, they began showing me there was a big, wide world outside Paris, Tennessee. I think it was then I began planning to try to be a part of it—a larger role than I could play in my hometown.

The Washington, DC, trip in 1959 introduced me to our nation's capital. But besides the many monuments we saw, I also remember visiting a mosque! Mom said she wanted us to see how people of other religions worshipped. Always a teacher, our mother was teaching us about another way to worship. However, we both knew she was not endorsing this belief. No way! We were staunch Christians.

Our 1961 New York trip included a few days in the Pennsylvania Dutch country, on the way to the Big Apple. Dad's cousin Dr. Joe Howard, grandson of the Civil War veteran of the same name who co-founded Howard & Jobe, was a professor of education at Kutztown State Teacher's College, in the heart of that picturesque region. I remember seeing Amish people with their horses and buggies.

I also remember our days in New York City itself. (Who wouldn't?) It was there and in Washington, DC, two years before, I began to notice how many different kinds of people there are! Paris, Tennessee, had little to prepare me for relating to people of different backgrounds. But my own parents, especially Mom, did. These family vacations were like big-time field trips.

Diversity has become a lifelong interest. I probably show my international students more attention than I should in the college classrooms where I teach today. Through meeting, knowing, and teaching people of different races, religions, and ethnicities, I have learned to appreciate the incredible variety of the human race. Diversity is a never-ending source of fascination. We are all threads in the human family.

Music and Words

One of the merit badges I earned as a Boy Scout was in music. When I was in the third grade (1953), I began piano lessons with Miss May Corum. Miss May was in her sixties or perhaps even older. To me, she seemed ancient. She lived on Dunlap Street in a red brick home that had been built before the Civil War. She had inherited it from her parents.

There were two pianos in her living room—an upright and a baby grand. She used them both for recitals, but my lessons were on the upright. She would sit somberly by my side, listening and watching intently as I played what she had assigned me to learn. If I hit a couple of wrong notes, she would "tap" my fingers with a long bamboo stick! If I made the same error again, the "tap" became a swat!

The idea to take piano lessons came naturally enough. Mom and her mother, Deda, had both been pianists. By this time, we were in our new home at 508 Jackson Street. Deda's old piano had been brought from Mt. Pleasant and sat proudly in our den. My musical accomplishments in the beginning were modest. I loved making sounds on the piano but hated practicing. (There is a big difference!) But my musical thread had begun.

I found Scouting more interesting than piano practice. I had become a Cub Scout. In the summer of 1954, I played center field in a Little League baseball team. (This was my only sustained attempt playing sports. I preferred riding my bicycle to being a part of a team.)

It's a miracle I stuck with the piano lessons. By the time I was eleven, however, I had become exasperated with Miss May's stern teaching methods. The last straw was when I totally forgot my recital piece. I played a few measures of the music, then my mind went blank! That's the only time it ever happened. It was embarrassing and scary, too. Where did that music go?

I quit piano lessons but continued to play music of my own choosing. I became a frequent customer of Tom Lonardo Piano Co. and his competitor—Sellers Leach. After about a year of this, Mom asked me one day if I would like to take lessons again. Thinking she meant Miss May, I said an emphatic "No!"

Mom replied quite calmly that there were other piano teachers besides her. This was a totally new idea: I could study piano without fearing a bamboo stick on my knuckles!

That's when Mrs. Covington came into my life. She was my last and best piano teacher in Paris. Miss May considered any music written after the Civil War to be modern! Mrs. Covington was more progressive. One of her students, whom I knew, was allowed to play Gershwin's "Rhapsody in Blue" for his recital.

That decided it for me. I would study with Mrs. Covington. Her home was on Blakemore Street, easily accessible by bicycle. I stayed with the piano lessons all through high school.

Marilyn also started piano lessons with Miss May when she was seven, and transitioned to Mrs. Covington along with me. She continued her studies through the middle of her junior year.

Her local career as a pianist overshadowed mine. By the time Marilyn was in high school she was accompanying at church and in town as well—children's choirs, community benefits, and two years as the pianist for the Olde Tyme Minstrel Show.

The "minstrel show" was an annual tradition staged by our beloved speech teacher "Miss Ruby" Krider (1904–1993) and her husband "Daddy Clem." The band had fine local musicians like Bill Crosswy (1925–1970), who directed the Grove junior and senior high bands, plus Tom Lonardo and Sellers Leach among others. I believe the show began in the 1940s.

The cast were all Grove High School students. (Remember, Grove did not begin token desegregation until the fall of 1962.) My sister was the minstrel pianist in 1964 and '65, its final two seasons! What is amazing about this, from the vantage point of 2012, is not that the show finally stopped in 1965, one year after the Civil Rights Act passed, but that it went on so long!

The "end men" and "end women" in the minstrel show wore blackface makeup. The show's dialogue contained jokes that today would be considered racist because they were delivered in so-called "Negro" dialect! Here's the kicker: the show was staged at the Paris Municipal Auditorium, which had been built on the corner of North Market and Rison Streets during the Depression as a WPA project.

If you followed Rison Street west across Market, it crossed the railroad tracks to one of Paris's larger African-American neighborhoods. If any black folks had wanted to attend the minstrel show from that area of town (highly unlikely!), the auditorium was within walking distance. The only "black faces" were in the cast, not the audience!

The final minstrel show was staged in May, 1965, a few months after the famed march from Selma to Montgomery, Alabama. The Voting Rights Act was passed later that year. And the Olde Tyme Minstrel Show in Paris, Tennessee, died! But Miss Ruby and Clem had plenty of other things to keep them busy.

Miss Ruby Krider, as she was called by almost everyone young and old—was originally from Hazel,

Kentucky, a state-line town between Paris and Murray, Kentucky. She came to Paris to attend Grove High School and while a student there, met and later married Clem Krider. The Kriders were an old established Paris family.

Many of Miss Ruby's students, known as Krider Kids, went on to become teachers, preachers, lawyers, college professors, and presidents, even professional actors. Tony-award winning actress Cherry Jones is perhaps the best-known Krider Kid on the national stage.

In Tennessee, one of her other female students, Nashville attorney Jayne Ann Woods, served as state commissioner of revenue in the 1970s, one of the first women to hold a cabinet-level post in state government.

Today, Paris has the Krider Performing Arts Center and an annual speech tournament named in her honor: the Ruby Krider Invitational. There is even a speech contest for students aged thirteen to eighteen called "Krider Idol"! Miss Ruby became nationally known as an outstanding high-school speech teacher.

After her retirement from Grove, Miss Ruby taught at nearby Murray State University (her undergraduate alma mater) and the University of Tennessee at Martin, about thirty-three miles west of Paris. She had also earned a master's degree from Northwestern University.

My cousins Bill and Jean were Krider Kids while at Grove High. I became one in the seventh grade (1957). Miss Ruby held classes at Atkins-Porter School as well as Grove by that time. When I entered Grove Junior High in 1958 as an eighth grader, I took speech lessons from her on Grove Hill. I was a Krider Kid through my junior year, 1961–-62.

The speech thread, much later in my life, became much larger and even more important, thanks to Miss Ruby.

Out West and Home Again

In the spring of 1962, I won the state oratorical contest in Johnson City. This qualified me to attend the National Forensic League's national competition in Missoula, Montana, in June. I was not the only one from Paris going to Montana that summer. There were four others, Jayne Ann Owens (later Woods) among them.

The carrot on the stick for me to win the state tournament was not a trophy, which I still have, but the trip west. I had been west of the Mississippi only once. My traveling thread,. which had begun with family trips, grew longer.

Miss Ruby and Clem took four of the five winners in their nine-passenger Ford station wagon. The trip took about a week. We crossed parts of Kentucky, Missouri,

Iowa, South Dakota, Wyoming, and finally Montana. The highlight of the trip west was Mount Rushmore. We also saw Yellowstone National Park.

The tournament was held at Montana State University in Missoula. Jim Rhea and I hiked up the mountain behind the campus. On a ledge high above the campus were some rocks painted white to spell the letter "M.". From the campus it looked like this was the very top. But when you got to the "M," you were not even halfway there.

I cannot remember whether we ever made it to the summit. The air was much thinner than back in Tennessee because we were in the Rockies—thousands of feet above sea level. Jim and I were both Eagle Scouts, but neither one of us was used to the altitude. (Jim's father, Dr. W. G. Rhea, delivered both my sister and me.)

The trip home took us through Idaho to Utah with beautiful Salt Lake City surrounded by mountains. I remember our hotel just across the street from the large Mormon Tabernacle. It was the highlight of the return trek. We left Salt Lake City and returned to Tennessee through Colorado, Missouri, Illinois, and Kentucky.

Marilyn also took speech from Miss Ruby in her freshman through senior years. She was a member of the National Forensic League and took part in some tournaments.

However, her main extracurricular activities were musical. She began clarinet lessons with Bill Crosswy in the sixth grade. Starting in the seventh grade (1961–1962), she played in the band for the next six years. In her senior year, she was historian for the band and received the Arion Award, given to the most outstanding band student every year.

Marilyn was active in other school activities. She was advertising manager for the Grove *Comet* (so named because it was founded in 1910—--the year Halley's Comet was visible across the United States). She was also a member of Future Teachers of America.

My journalistic career began in eighth grade when I was asked by Miss Aline Lowry, faculty advisor for the *Comet*, to cover stories for my grade. I stayed on the staff all through high school, becoming editor my senior year.

For some strange reason, I never thought of this leading to any sort of career. Ironically, since high school I have worked as a journalist, advertising copywriter, jingle writer, and copy editor in Christian book publishing. Now, at age sixty-six, I'm writing this book. God does have a sense of humor!

Marilyn and I were both "TK"s—teacher's kids! This had a profound effect on us then and later. Today, I am a college professor and my sister, for many years before her retirement, was assistant director of her church's daycare center in Easley, South Carolina.

Our mother began teaching in Murfreesboro in 1940, but quit after one year to marry my father. In 1956, she returned to the classroom at Atkins-Porter Elementary School to teach seventh-grade geography. I was in the sixth grade. So next year, it was Mom for geography!

It was a long, awkward year for both of us! I could never decide what to call her. Mostly, I kept quiet. This suited Mom just fine! I love geography and my mother. But one year of having both in the same class was enough!

Saving Howard & Jobe

After two years teaching geography at A-P, Mom moved to Grove High and became the senior English teacher. In 1962, she left teaching to work with my father in the store.

Marilyn and I did not know it then, but Mom's return to teaching was not just for professional fulfillment. We needed the extra money! Howard & Jobe was going through some difficult years.

After Grandpa Horace died in late 1953, the once-solid partnership between my dad and my uncle Howard began to fray around the edges. My uncle's health was slowly failing but none of us knew it, probably not even him.

Uncle Howard behaved more and more erratically. He was absent more than present in the family business. However, he continued to draw his salary, his half of the partnership. This put extra pressure on my father and on our family. My parents tried to shield my sister and me from all this. But there were tell-tale signs.

Mom had just gotten her monthly school paycheck one Friday afternoon. She took us directly to another department store, which was Howard & Jobe's competitor. She bought several items of clothing for both of us. I was thrilled by my new clothes and wanted to go by our store to show them to Dad.

Mom said, "No, it will just hurt his feelings!"

I asked why. She told me the store was not doing that well.

Dad told me in 1960, the last year he and Uncle Howard were still partners, Howard & Jobe made a profit of only $600 for the entire year! Our old family store was going downhill! Word travels fast in a small town.

In 1961, Uncle Howard suffered a stroke and became unable to work. He was forced to retire at age sixty. Mom and Dad saw this as an opportunity and bought his share of the business. Mom quit teaching the next year to become Dad's business partner.

This saved Howard & Jobe and our family's fortunes with it. My sister once said, "Mom saved that store!" It also preserved her health.

The combination of teaching and the added financial pressure of Howard & Jobe's woes took its toll on Mom's body. On a family vacation trip to New York in 1961, she complained of severe abdominal pain. Not wanting to go to a strange hospital in a part of the country we did not know, she prevailed upon Dad to drive us home.

At that point, we were in western New York State, a good three days from Paris. Marilyn and I sat in the front seat while Mom lay across the back seat with every agonizing mile. Dad drove us home through Ohio and Kentucky. Arriving in Paris, he took her straight to Henry County General Hospital.

Mom had to have her gall bladder removed. The surgery was successful. However, my sister says that when they wheeled Mom out of the operating room, still sedated, Dad cried! Marilyn says it's the only time she ever saw him cry! (The only other time was on his deathbed when he was ninety-two.)

In 1963, when Mom was forty-four, she was diagnosed with diabetes, something she lived with until she died in 1995! I will always believe many of her health problems stemmed from these stressful years before she and Dad took over the store. But Mom was not a whiner or a quitter! She was a lot tougher than I gave her credit for.

Also in the background of this family drama was the house—Mom's pride and joy. They had planned to retire in that big house at 508 Jackson Street. It was not to be. In May, 1969, while I was in Nashville working in advertising and Marilyn was a student at Furman University in Greenville, South Carolina, Mom and Dad announced the Jobe "mansion" had been sold.

They rented a large three-bedroom, two-bath house in another part of town for about two more years. It was here my sister's wedding was held in 1970. In 1971, they rented an apartment downtown within walking distance of both the store and First Baptist Church. The apartment was actually across the street from the church.

Many years later, our parents told us that during the store's bad years in the late 1950s, they had been able to pay only the *interest* on the house note, nothing more! Mom said, of their final earthly home—202 Camille Street in Easley, South Carolina—a block away from Marilyn, Jack, and the grandkids, Heather and Brian—that if they had built a house of more modest dimensions in Paris like the Easley home, they would still have it.

How did Mom save Howard & Jobe? We saw a side of her we had never seen before. The store had a nice modern exterior thanks to the 1951 remodeling. However, the interior needed some work. Mom and Dad took over a business heavily in debt with low cash flow and a diminished reputation. Success was anything but guaranteed.

Many people who are not familiar with retailing imagine it's easy. Just put the merchandise on the shelves, open the doors, and take your customers' money as they rush to buy. Nothing could be further from the truth. Retail is as dog-eat-dog as any other business.

Howard & Jobe had been a fixture in Paris for sixty years—since 1901. But the operative rule in any business is giving the customer what he or she wants when that customer wants it! Howard & Jobe was apparently perceived as old-fashioned—a great store whose time had come and gone!

Mom made some changes that, over time, showed their customers the old store still had what it took! She did some redecorating. Drab walls suddenly sparkled with bright colors—orange, always a popular color in Tennessee because of the UT Vols—and other lively hues.

She installed a sound system, and brought their record player from home and connected it to the speakers. Music played softly throughout the store, adding to the atmosphere.

These changes created an attractive ambience for shopping. Mom and Dad expanded the gift-wrapping department and offered it free. This especially helped boost sales between Thanksgiving and New Year's. Howard & Jobe traditionally made one-third of its annual profit during this six-week period—as did most other retail businesses.

My parents closely examined the profitability of every line of merchandise. Some items proved to be duds. Others were hits. The duds got ditched. The hits got more space and more advertising. A turnaround was underway. Howard & Jobe entered the 1970s as one of the leading stores in Paris once again.

In 1975, after several years in Nashville and Atlanta, I returned home to attend graduate school at nearby Murray State University in Kentucky. I worked three days a week for the store.

One of my duties was advertising, something I had done professionally for several years. In 1976, I created an ad campaign for the store's seventy-fifth anniversary—"We Couldn't Have Done it Without You."

To tell the truth, Howard & Jobe couldn't have done it without Mom! No one knew this better than Dad! My mother had helped to give new life to a thread of commerce that had been a part of Paris since 1901. Even though I have made my living differently, Howard & Jobe will always be an important thread in the fabric of my life.

Band and Paper Days

The piano was not my only musical outlet. About the time Marilyn began clarinet lessons (1960), I took drum lessons from Bill Crosswy during the summer. The Grove High Band desperately needed drummers and, since they did not need pianists, I decided to join the drum line.

I was never a threat to any other drummers, but did have a good time during my four years in the band. For this teenaged boy, being in the band was fun. Besides getting to wear a uniform and march, I had choice seats for the games and a good view of the majorettes!

Sometime during my junior year, I began to compose little pieces. I wrote a fanfare and asked Mr. Crosswy for help, which he generously gave, arranging it for the band. He taught me the fundamentals of instruments and their transposition to different keys in one marathon session during the final week of classes. He said if

I could successfully orchestrate my brief "Gridiron Fanfare" that summer, the band would play it in the fall.

I worked very hard for much of that summer on my little "symphony." True to his word, that fall Mr. Crosswy had the band play it to kick off the opening home game. They even announced it as my own composition.

Looking back on this event decades later, I owe most of the sound of my fanfare to the famous film composer Miklos Rozsa (1907–1995), whose scores for *"Ben-Hur"* (1959) and another Charlton Heston epic *"El Cid"* (1961) I loved from the first time I saw the films in a theater! "Imitation is the sincerest form of flattery."

Look out, Music World, here I come! It didn't work out that way, but I have had fun writing music and getting it heard over the years. I even published two songs, over two decades apart.

Bill Crosswy, our much-loved band director at Grove Junior and Senior High, was diagnosed with lung cancer in the late 1960s. He died July 23, 1970, shortly after his forty-fifth birthday. It was wonderful, caring teachers like him, Miss Ruby Krider and our Mom who inspired my sister and me to follow their examples.

My senior year was busy as usual with band, editing the *Comet*, and schoolwork. I had chosen to drop out of speech after my junior year when I won the state tournament. The trip to Montana capped my career as a Krider Kid. But Miss Ruby would make one more important appearance in my life years later—one that changed my life.

In May, 1963, I finally graduated from Grove High School. I had been hired by the P-I as a reporter and photographer. (I had also taken photos for the *Comet*.) Paris had two daily newspapers when I was younger, but by this time only the P-I remained. Newspapers today are an endangered species because of competition from the Internet.

I spent that summer writing stories and taking pictures for the P-I. I remember my salary—very small. In addition, I was expected to dress like a reporter. In 1963, this meant a white shirt and tie. I was blessed our store sold these items! I could not have afforded them on my meager salary. However, I got some good journalistic experience that would come in handy later.

The combined threads of words and music from my hometown beginnings have created a song that defines my life even now—almost half a century later. And the threads go on…

Sister Story

Marilyn graduated from Grove High in 1967. Hers was one of the last classes to graduate from the old school on Grove Hill. Despite much opposition from rural areas, the Henry County Board of Education had voted to close several high schools throughout the county, including Grove. In 1969, a new consolidated Henry County High School opened in eastern Paris. Grove became a junior high.

This change, together with civil rights, brought the end of an era in local education. The new high school was desegregated. Because of consolidation, it could offer more of everything than any of the old county high schools, even Grove.

Marilyn entered Furman University in Greenville, South Carolina, in the fall of 1967. Our pastor's wife, Joy Owen, was a graduate of this Baptist school and encouraged Marilyn to go there. She majored in elementary education.

Marilyn's roommate, Jane Hendricks, introduced her to her brother Jack at a football game on Thanksgiving weekend. Jack was in the air force and home on leave. They began dating. A few months later, he proposed and Marilyn accepted.

The Vietnam War was raging overseas. In 1969, Jack was ordered to an air force base in Thailand, not far from the Mekong River. He was a mechanic and did not fly. But he was still in harm's way.

Marilyn kept busy with schoolwork. She also worked a part-time job on the switchboard at the university, something she had also done back in Paris at Henry County General Hospital her senior year. And she prayed a lot for Jack.

Jack was away a long time, but the two were finally reunited when he returned safely from Thailand. They planned their wedding for September 7, 1970: Mom and Dad's twenty-ninth anniversary.

The wedding was held at their home on Hillcrest Drive. It was a very hot day. The ceremony was performed by our pastor, Brother Carroll C. Owen, in the back yard while everyone tried to stay cool, without much success.

Their honeymoon was also a trip to their new home: Minot, North Dakota! Jack still had six months left to serve Uncle Sam. He was assigned to Minot Air Force Base. His enlistment ended in February, 1971.

Marilyn had two major adjustments: marriage and the brutal North Dakota winter! Managing the first was much easier than the second. But they survived. When Jack was finally a civilian again, they returned to Greenville where they rented an apartment. Marilyn finished her senior year and graduated from Furman.

Jack had attended a local technical college and used that schooling and his air force experience to get a job with the telephone company—at that time called Southern Bell. He ended up as an installer and stayed with "Ma Bell" the rest of his career.

In January, 1975, my sister gave birth to their first child—Heather Elizabeth Hendricks. She was joined by her brother, Matthew Brian, in February, 1978.

Heather and Brian both graduated from high school in Easley, where Marilyn and Jack had bought a home. Easley is a bedroom community in Pickens County, just west of Greenville. Jack's parents lived outside town. His mother was a graduate of Furman and a teacher. His father was a World War II veteran and a businessman.

Marilyn worked for many years as the assistant director at her church's daycare center. She also taught piano at home, keeping alive a family musical tradition going back to her grandmother Deda.

After high school, Heather majored in public administration and graduated from Samford University in Birmingham, Alabama. Brian got a degree in forestry from Clemson University near Easley. At Samford, Heather met her future husband, Bill Vinson, who was from the Atlanta area. They were married in December, 1996.

The Vinsons live in the Raleigh, North Carolina, area where Heather is a high-school teacher. Bill is the family "computer geek," and has worked in that industry since graduating from Samford in the mid-1990s, along with Heather. They have two young sons—my great-nephews, Bennett (called Ben!) and Ian Joss Vinson.

By the mid-1990s, Jack's health had begun to fail. He became unable to work and retired. Jack died on December 31, 2001. He had just turned fifty-five.

During this time, Brian became a de facto caregiver for his parents, first for his father and later for his mother, my sister. Brian decided to return to school and become a registered nurse. Today, he works at a large Greenville hospital.

On Monday, August 8, 2011, while I was finishing work on this manuscript, Heather called with the sad news that her mother Marilyn had passed away suddenly at home in Easley. My son Josh and I had just visited Marilyn and her son (my nephew) Brian there a few weeks before.

Marilyn endured several years of poor health, but even so, her sudden departure from this life took us all by surprise. Her funeral (which she planned years before) was a time of praise and worship to her Lord and Savior. Now she is with Him, her parents, her husband,

Jack, and other members of both families, and she is totally healed!

Someday, we will all be reunited in glory and all our life threads will be woven together in an eternal pattern!

Retirement and Beyond

In 1979, my parents sold Howard & Jobe to a Paris couple they had known for many years. They had purchased a condominium in Vero Beach, Florida, in 1974. During the years in between, they made frequent trips to their Florida place, especially in the winter.

They had planned to spend their final years in the Sunshine State. However, the Lord intervened in a most unexpected way. Mom and Dad had closed out their Paris apartment. They finished moving one last truckload into their condo the Friday before Labor Day, 1979. On Sunday, local media warned: Hurricane David was closing in on Vero Beach. All residents were ordered to evacuate!

My parents had barely settled into their new home and now they had to leave it. They drove in bumper-to-bumper traffic across the state to Florida's west coast. When they returned on Tuesday, their second-story condo had water damage—about 18 inches! (The third floor had been totally wiped out by the hurricane!)

Mom and Dad had been advised by several knowledgeable persons when they bought their condo in 1974 to purchase hurricane insurance. The events of Labor Day weekend made them glad they did! They rented an apartment for the next several months while their condo was being rebuilt.

After the condo was finished, Mom and Dad decided to sell it and move inland away from the path of hurricanes. They did not want to return to Paris because both wanted a change of scenery in their last years. So they moved to Easley, South Carolina, and bought a house near Marilyn, Jack, and their family. The Carolina Piedmont climate was also a little warmer than Paris and this suited my parents.

They joined First Baptist Church and Mom began teaching a Sunday School class once again. The Easley years were good ones. They were able to see Heather and Brian grow up. And I got in the habit of visiting them there, which was much closer than Florida!

Mom became a senior world traveler. In 1982, she went to Israel with a tour group. I remember all the photos she brought back. It was a life-changing experience. In the summer of 1984, she went with another tour group to Oberammergau, Germany, to see a passion play that had been performed there for 350 years, since 1634! They also stopped in Vienna, Austria, at one time the classical music capital of the world!

On one of these trips, Mom had an unpleasant experience at the airport in Amsterdam. For some unknown reason, a security computer selected her as worthy of being searched! Apparently, they thought she might be a terrorist!

Mom was mad of course, but could do nothing as she and her luggage were searched by customs officials! They found nothing incriminating. In the post- 9/11 world of today, this may seem routine, but when it happened to my mother, it was just plain weird!

Mom had lived with diabetes for over thirty years. Since moving to Easley, she had had surgery on her feet and for cataracts. In spring, 1995, she was diagnosed with female-related cancer. She had surgery to have it removed.

The surgery was successful, but the incision became infected. She developed blood poisoning. Her kidneys began to fail. Other major complications followed. It was the beginning of the end. After several weeks in the Easley hospital, Mom finally went home to be with her Lord Jesus on July 31, 1995. She was seventy-six. My parents had been married almost fifty-four years.

The funeral was at First Baptist Church in Easley. Her remains were placed in a mausoleum in a local cemetery. She and Dad had planned everything about their respective departures. Another space next to Mom's was ready for Dad.

He lived on in the house on Camille Street for a few months, but the next year, 1996, he moved into assisted living on the advice of his doctor. I visited him several times a year as my schedule would permit. Marilyn took good care of him, as he was just across town. She visited him almost daily.

On the afternoon of April 6, 1999, when he was ninety-two years old, Dad was waiting at the front entrance for Marilyn to meet him. He was the oldest male resident in the assisted-living facility. A group of elderly women came to the front door. Marilyn pulled up in her car.

A Southern gentleman to the end, Dad turned to hold the door for them. This would be one of his last conscious acts on earth. A bone in his hip gave way and he fell. At the hospital, they performed hip-replacement surgery. He contracted pneumonia. His condition worsened. After several days on a ventilator, his doctor asked Marilyn if they should invoke Dad's living will.

This document stated if he could only be kept alive by artificial means and there was no hope of a better quality of life without life support, that it be disconnected. This was done early in the evening of Saturday, April 17, with my sister's consent.

He lived through the night, every breath a struggle. I arrived at his hospital bed early Sunday morning, summoned by my sister. We both watched him take his last breaths before he slipped away.

I will always remember saying good-bye to him, thanking him for being such a good father. I was not sure he understood. Then I saw tears flow out of both closed eyes and down his cheeks. He was responding the only way he could!

Dad had met Mom on a Friday in March, 1940 at First Baptist Church in Paris. Now on a Sunday in April, 1999, they met again in an eternal place where they would never grow old and feeble, where time is no more!

Two days later, on April 20, my father was buried in the mausoleum next to his beloved bride. Now I know why author Tom Brokaw titled his best-selling book *The Greatest Generation*. Both of our parents were part of that generation and they were the greatest!

No, they weren't perfect. But they knew One who is, and introduced Him to me and my sister. Most of all, I love them for that! One day in heaven, we will all be together again. I will meet some of my ancestors for the first time. There will be no pain, no sorrow, and no tears. "God shall wipe every tear from their eyes" (Revelation 7:17). Our life threads will last forever.

Part Four:

My Own Weave

"Trust in the Lord with all your heart; and do not lean on your own understanding"

(Proverbs 3:5).

In the spring of 1963, the year I graduated from Grove High School, I saw a movie at the Capitol Theatre in Paris that changed my life: *"To Kill a Mockingbird"*. I had read the book when it came out in 1960. The movie and the book have since become classics.

The images on the screen touched some deep places inside me. For one thing, Maycomb, Harper Lee's fictional small Southern town, in many ways resembled Paris, even though the story took place years before I was born.

The quiet, gentle wisdom of Atticus Finch, as portrayed by Gregory Peck, reminded me of my dad. Even Atticus's white suit reminded me of another prominent Parisian, attorney Aaron Brown, who was mayor for several years. I am friends with his son Jerry, who is also an adjunct professor in Nashville.

A civil-rights leader once said, "Martin Luther King did not just liberate black people; he liberated white people, too."

"*To Kill a Mockingbird*" helped begin my own liberation from racism. I had many strong bottled-up emotions about all the anger and hatred swirling around me. These angry feelings rubbed off on me! I was desperate to leave home—in more ways than one. I had been accepted as a student at Nashville's George Peabody College for Teachers. I would major in music.

I did not expect Nashville's racial relations to be much different but at least there I would not be part of a prominent family whose business kept us constantly in the public eye. I have always fled the limelight. Part of the appeal of urban living for me is its anonymity.

The choice of Nashville as the location of my college was a natural. Mom was from Mt. Pleasant in Maury County, some fifty miles to the south. Childhood trips to visit Deda had often included a side trip to Music City.

Something happened in the late 1950s that brought me to Nashville more often than to Mt. Pleasant to see Deda. I got braces on my teeth! The orthodontist was in downtown Nashville. From 1957 to 1961, we made monthly trips to get the braces tightened. After the braces came off, I had to wear a retainer. This meant more trips to Nashville.

While the "orthodontics" part of the trip was not fun, going to Nashville for the day was! Most department stores were downtown then. Suburban shopping malls were in the future. After my orthodontist visit, Mom would let me visit the record department of a store for a while.

In those days, some stores had a listening booth. It was meant to "try out " a record before you bought it. I abused this privilege on many occasions, monopolizing the booth with movie soundtracks. More than once, a clerk demanded I leave if I was not going to buy a record!

I fell in love with music, not through piano lessons or music in church, but hearing many glorious background scores at the Capitol Theatre in downtown Paris, and sometimes the Sundown and Sky-Vue Drive-ins, too. I went to the movies every chance I got. I loved all kinds of films, but the so-called "spear-and-sandal" epics, most of them biblically based, really captured my imagination: *The Robe, The Ten Commandments,* and especially *Ben-Hur*.

Listening to a soundtrack album in a downtown Nashville department store fired my imagination and nourished my soul! How dare that mean woman make me leave!? If I had had enough money, I would have bought every soundtrack in the place. I planned to major in music in college. I had vague plans of going to Hollywood someday and writing music for the movies.

I received my diploma from Grove High, and worked that summer as a reporter and photographer for the Paris daily newspaper. By late August, I was ready to attend George Peabody College for Teachers in Nashville.

The last week of August was freshman orientation week. We were taken on a tour of the Hermitage, where President Andrew Jackson once lived. Among the sights we saw were slave cabins—the first such dwellings I had ever seen. Ironically, that was also the week of the famed March on Washington. A quarter of a million people crowded into the mall in front of the Lincoln Memorial to hear numerous speakers on August 28.

Late that afternoon, Dr. Martin Luther King, Jr., delivered his "I Have a Dream" speech, since honored as one of the greatest speeches ever given by an American. Years later, I would use a videotape of his speech in some of my public speaking classes. At the time, I saw an excerpt on television and knew "I Have a Dream" was special.

I remember hearing someone in Paris in the early 1960s say something like this: "Our colored people are all right; but heaven help us if one of those outside agitators like Martin Luther King comes to town!" Through millions of television screens on August 28, 1963, Dr. King finally *did come* to Paris, Nashville, Memphis, Birmingham, Atlanta, New York, Chicago, Los Angeles—and the entire world.

The civil-rights movement changed America and the world. In a very small way, my family was part of that—employing Dave Travis so he could lead the local NAACP without fear of being fired; my mother introducing me to Sidney Poitier's work in films; my sister sharing a classroom with Wilson Kendall, whose mother worked for our family business. And my parents always leading by example as they taught us how to get along with everyone.

No, these were not dramatic, world-shaking events. But they helped to shape my worldview and open my mind to new possibilities. I think our family was typical of millions of others in the South—black and white—who shared a simple, decent desire to get along with each other despite the barriers imposed by segregation. That is one of the "common threads" in this book.

In the fall of 1963, I began music studies at George Peabody College for Teachers in Nashville. This included piano lessons with Mr. Werner Zepernick. He had emigrated from Germany after World War II and spoke with a thick accent. I guess I did, too, but mine was familiar! No accent ever sounds strange to the one who speaks it!

Peabody had a unique arrangement with neighboring Vanderbilt University called the Joint University Band. Most of the musicians were Peabody music majors.

Funding and the football team came from Vandy. Once again, I became a part of the drum line and stayed there for two years. It was a time for musical threads.

A Time to Kill and a Time to Heal

On a warm, sunny day in 1963, President John F. Kennedy visited Nashville. His motorcade made its way out West End Avenue to Vanderbilt's Dudley Stadium. Some friends and I watched from the crowd. President Kennedy was in an open car, standing and waving to everyone. I remember thinking how vulnerable he looked in that open car and how easy it would be for someone to take aim at him from the crowd!

Then on Friday, November 22, I was eating lunch in the Peabody College cafeteria with some fellow music majors before our 1:00 p.m. theory class. Someone on the loudspeaker made a strange announcement: "The president has been shot in Dallas, Texas. That's all we know."

Some of us laughed it off as a bad joke. We went on to class, which was taught by Professor Zepernick. At about 1:30, there was a knock on the door. Mr. Zepernick excused himself. In a minute he returned and his face said it all. In a quiet voice, he said, " The president has died. Class is dismissed."

As I returned to my dorm room, the campus was eerily quiet. There was only one television set for students in the three-story dorm—in the main lobby. A large crowd gathered around it as events unfolded in Dallas. I remember feeling sad and afraid all at the same time.

The last few years leading up to this had been full of violence—because of civil rights. Now violence had snuffed out our president. Kennedy had already introduced his Civil Rights Bill in Congress earlier that year. It was stalled in Congress due to a Southern filibuster, but the movement in the South continued.

In 1961, many of the Freedom Riders had left Nashville, headed south for Alabama. One bus was firebombed when they arrived. The year before that, Nashville had made national headlines as the site of the downtown sit-ins. Music City had played an important role in the movement.

But I doubt that was on anyone's mind as we huddled around the dormitory's television set the evening of November 22, 1963. Our president was dead at the hands of an assassin. Most of us were numb.

This tragedy was not received the same way at all American colleges and universities. On many Southern campuses, including the University of Tennessee in Knoxville, there was cheering, horn-blowing, and signs celebrating the death of "our nigger-loving president"!

We usually had band practice on Friday afternoon, but this Friday I went to my room for a nap. Our national tragedy left me tired and depressed! On Saturday morning, I made my way to the lobby to the television. I arrived moments after Jack Ruby had shot Lee Harvey Oswald, believed to have been President Kennedy's assassin! The crowd gathered around the TV was in an uproar!

Vanderbilt had a home game that afternoon. I reported to the band room. Because of the assassination, the prepared half-time show had been replaced at the last minute. We marched onto the field at half-time, a solemn drum cadence our only music. We got into position and played "The Star-Spangled Banner" and "Hail to the Chief." Flags were at half staff as they were across the country and much of the world.

I will always remember watching the president's funeral on television Monday. I think classes were cancelled as they were in most colleges across the nation. The entire weekend had been like a long freeze-frame.

One thing I do remember from that long weekend: one of the networks kept playing video of our major symphony orchestras performing classical music deemed appropriate for the solemn occasion. That was when I first heard Brahms's *"A German Requiem"* and fell in love with it. Brahms's music was a thread of comfort to help heal the wounds of the nation.

The rest of my freshman year was uneventful. I studied, not as much as I should, and took advantage of "city life" when I could. This included concerts by the Nashville Symphony, which I got to hear free because I had volunteered to usher. They used Peabody music majors. It was great!

I do not remember this, but Mom told me when I was a preschooler, she would play recordings of composers like Tchaikovsky and Rachmaninoff while I crawled around the living room. I guess the music somehow got into me. Mom had been introduced to classical music one summer while in college. She won a scholarship to Chautauqua, New York, on Lake Erie. It was there she first heard a live symphony orchestra.

When school ended, I returned to the *P-I* for the summer of 1964. It was an exciting time to be in the news business, especially in the South because of civil rights. The Civil-Rights Act was finally passed by Congress and signed by President Johnson! Change was in the air!

That fall I returned to the band. They sent us to Birmingham when Vanderbilt played the University of Alabama. I remember after the game, some of us went out on the town. When I returned to our hotel there was much talk about what had happened to Johnny (not his real name), the band's first and only black member.

Walking back to the hotel with two or three other bandsmen—all white—a passing car had slowed, a loud N-word was heard, and a brick was hurled in Johnny's direction! It missed him and the other bandsmen, thank goodness! I do not remember whether Vanderbilt won or lost the game, but I do not think this had anything to do with the brick-throwing incident.

We had taken the train from Nashville to Birmingham. On Sunday morning as we were riding the rails back to Tennessee, someone gasped and pointed out the coach's window. There on the top of a steep hill stood three blackened, burned crosses! The Ku Klux Klan must have had a meeting!

In my sophomore year, I joined the staff of the school paper and became friends with the editor Danny Lee. One day, Danny came by and asked if I wanted to go with him downtown to apply for work at the *Tennessean*. I was not keen on the idea, but went along anyway and filled out an application.

When school was over, I returned to Paris. One Friday evening early in June, I was at a friend's house when the phone rang. It was Dad. He said to call a number (which he had written down) in Nashville at once. It was the *Tennessean*! They wanted me in Nashville for a job interview!

I had to get Mom to drive me there on Monday. They offered me a job as a reporter. My experience with the P-I had apparently gotten their attention. I was so blinded by the glamour of working for a big-city newspaper I conveniently overlooked the low salary: $65 per week for forty hours! This amounted to $1.25 a hour. It was 1965, but this amount was still only minimum wage for the times.

I needed a car to keep the job. My parents helped me purchase a used 1962 Chevrolet two-door sedan from a local lot. It was green, had air-conditioning, automatic transmission, and low mileage. Mom and Dad loaned me the money to buy it on the condition I pay them back with my earnings. I think I paid only about half the money back.

I was nineteen years old and working for a major metropolitan daily newspaper! And I had a car! Never mind that I made only minimum wage and wore shirts and ties from the family store. At last I had arrived—or so I thought.

They assigned me to write features articles. I also conducted interviews and went "on location" sometimes with a photographer. I have some good memories from this job. I stayed with it as fall semester began. I worked a full forty hours per week and took twelve hours of classes.

One person I remember fondly from those six months at the *Tennessean* was Bill Reed, the religion editor. He was a middle-aged black man, Nashville native, and a graduate of Fisk University. (I had not yet met Coach Ben, also a Fiskite.) My desk was right in front of his. Bill Reed became my friend and mentor. I was only nineteen and pretty "green" so I really needed some help.

Besides covering local religious news, Bill wrote a weekly column, which always ran on Monday: "A Reporter Goes to Church." One day he told me he would be out for about a month for minor surgery. He asked if I would write his weekly column for him. I was thrilled!

He said he would set up the churches in advance. All I had to do was go to each one on a given Sunday morning and report on the worship service. I asked him to send me to some black churches, which he was glad to do.

I remember a sense of adventure, as I had never attended an African-American church in my life. Later, I heard a famous quote by Dr. Martin Luther King, Jr.: "Eleven o'clock on Sunday morning is the most segregated hour in America."

Bill sent me to all kinds of churches, from a poor inner-city congregation to an affluent congregation high on a hill overlooking Tennessee State University. (I had no way to know I would be teaching there thirty-three years later.)

The upper-crust church near TSU showed me a side of black life in Nashville I had been unaware of: some black folks had more money than many whites! The cars out front were mostly shiny, late-model gas guzzlers! To a white boy from Paris, Tennessee, this was all new!

The people at all four African-American churches went out of their way to welcome me. Of course a cynic might say it was because I was with the "press." I think it was more. These good people were simply extending their Christian hospitality to a young guest in their church. In every church, mine was the only white face. When these folks made me feel at home, it did not matter!

Their kindness left a lasting impression on me, and no doubt contributed to the *"To Kill a Mockingbird"* effect: liberation from the shackles of segregation. I will always be grateful to Bill Reed for allowing me to cover for him. It became much more than a work assignment. I thanked him effusively when he returned to the city room.

These church visits were a highlight of my brief career at the *Tennessean*. I also wrote feature articles and conducted interviews. One person I interviewed was the famous concert violinist Yehudi Menuhin!

However, I paid more attention to the job than school and my grades began to show it. Since my parents were paying for my education and because the newspaper job paid only minimum wage, when fall grades came out, they insisted I quit the paper and get another job on campus. Reluctantly, I exchanged my newspaper job for the food line in the cafeteria. This did not pay any money but I got two free meals a day! I stayed with this job for a long time.

My main source of friendship and fun during my college days was Phi Mu Alpha Sinfonia, a national professional music fraternity. Peabody's chapter Gamma Psi was one of the oldest in the country. They even had their own fraternity house, a rarity for a professional music fraternity. (Peabody had some Greek organizations but none of them had national affiliations.)

I joined Phi Mu Alpha during my freshman year and stayed throughout my entire four years, even after changing my major twice. I switched from music to English as a sophomore and later to an area major in social studies with an English minor. I have always loved history and words so this was the best fit. But music would always be an important part of my life.

A number of music majors were fun to be around. I especially remember one girl, an outstanding concert pianist in the making whose family had come to Nashville from China. Her roommate was from a small Middle Tennessee town. The two used to go downtown, stand on opposite street corners, point at each other and shout:

"Capitalist pig! Capitalist pig!"

"Communist dog! Communist dog!"

They would do this at the top of their lungs for several minutes, then abruptly vanish! It always drew a crowd!

Peabody was on the quarter system until about 1965–66 when the school switched to semesters, to better coordinate with Vanderbilt. Many Peabody students took classes at Vandy and vice versa. The Joint University Band was only one of several shared programs. Another was the Joint University Library. In 1979, Vanderbilt merged with Peabody after my alma mater had endured many bad fiscal years. This was a good academic match.

The summer of 1965, I needed an inexpensive place to stay because my take-home pay at the newspaper was $53.54 a week. The Phi Mu Alpha house charged only $20 a month so I moved there for the summer. I shared a room with another Sinfonian. It was a fun place to live—with other "crazy" music majors! I moved back into the frat house for the summer of 1966 and my senior year.

In the summer of 1966, I landed a part-time summer job with the Nashville Area Chamber of Commerce. I had met Ed Shea, their executive V-P, through my job at the *Tennessean*. He hired me as a summer intern in advertising and public relations. I worked twenty hours a week. It was fascinating work, if not lucrative. I lived in the Phi Mu Alpha house once again.

During my junior year, I returned to the dorm and had a Jewish roommate. He had moved with his family from New York City to Nashville when he was in the ninth grade. He often asked me things such as, "Are you sure you're not a Jew?"

I asked "Why?"

"Because," he said, "you think like we do!"

Now, years later, I know why he said that. I am, in fact, part Jewish.

In the November elections of 1966, I voted for the first time. (I had turned twenty-one a few weeks before, on October 17.) I remember voting for Howard Baker for the US Senate. I had been old enough to fight for my country since I was eighteen. Somehow, this did not seem fair! The legal age of adulthood is now eighteen, except for drinking in many states. I believe this is a big improvement.

I had a few dates here and there, but no serious girlfriend. I was too busy, and probably too shy for a serious relationship. There was a lovely young woman—a brunette two years older than I was—for whom I carried a torch a long time. She was a music major and engaged to a Vanderbilt student from her hometown.

In the background of my college years—especially from 1965 to graduation in 1967—was the Vietnam War. As America's involvement grew, so did the antiwar movement. Peabody students were very much aware of this, as some of our international students were Vietnamese. One female student—the only other from Paris besides me—later married one of them!

By 1967, I was in the last semester of my quest for a college degree. I had been given a student deferment as a freshman, even though I had registered for the draft when I turned eighteen, as the law required. Now, with graduation staring me in the face, I realized I would soon lose this deferment.

I graduated in June and took a job with the Nashville Children's Museum (now called Adventure Science Center). I rented a one-bedroom apartment not far for the Peabody campus and continued to spend time there when I could.

But looming over everything was the Vietnam War—half a world away, and yet as close as your television set. The Vietnam War was America's first war to be extensively covered by television and this in time helped to turn the public against it.

I do not remember having strong feelings for or against the war, but when I lost my student deferment the summer of 1967, my view about the war crystallized. I was dead-set against it! In August, I received my draft notice. I quit the museum job, certain I was bound for Vietnam. On the advice of some friends, I took the entrance exam for the Navy Officer Candidate School. I did not pass the exam—a new experience!

I had had severe asthma as a child but the attacks gradually subsided by the time I was twelve. However, I had one final attack when I was home for Christmas my freshman year at Peabody. This ailment proved to be a blessing in disguise.

My dad advised me to see Dr. John Neumann, our family doctor. Dr. Neumann was a World War II veteran like Dad, having served in the army. I remember him making house calls when I was home with asthma as a child, sitting by my bedside telling stories of WWII!

I asked Dr. Neumann what could be done. He wrote a letter for me that greatly exaggerated the extent of my childhood asthma. His letter was accepted by the military authorities and I did not have to go. Looking back on this, I have mixed feelings about my doctor's unethical letter. But Vietnam is one war I'm glad I missed!

In September, after being exempted from military service, I returned to Nashville and within a few days landed a job as an advertising agency copywriter. It was not my journalistic experience that got my foot in the door, but some silly columns I had written for the Peabody College newspaper.

My salary was $500 a month, $6,000 a year. I found a furnished apartment in the upstairs of a private home a block off West End Avenue for $75 a month. (Remember, this was 1967!) The '62 Chevy still ran well and I learned about commuting. Several late arrivals to the office helped me learn!

The agency's offices were downtown on Church Street next to the Life and Casualty Tower. Built in 1955, the L & C Tower was the tallest building in Nashville at thirty-one stories. There was an observation deck on top. Our modest three-story building was next door. The agency was on the second floor.

Our creative director was a native of Birmingham, Alabama, but had studied at a prestigious art school in Los Angeles! (He had hired me and was my immediate superior.) There were two other copywriters—both women—and a couple of art directors. There were also account executives, a production manager, a media buyer, and a secretary or two. It was a small shop, almost like a family. I began to learn about the world of advertising.

Our accounts were almost all local—a bank, a furniture store, a meat-packing company, and the city's public electric utility among others. I wrote newspaper ads, brochures, and radio and television commercials.

I was tutored in producing the broadcast spots and worked with some very talented, experienced people: announcers, sound engineers, and voice-over talent that included actors, actresses, and so forth. They let me go to a television station to produce these ads. I was enthralled!

We had gotten our first television set in the fall of 1953, in the big new house at 508 Jackson Street. It was a twenty-one-inch black-and-white unit that sat in a corner in our den. When homework was done, my sister and I were allowed to watch, provided we could agree on what! Marilyn also had a portable radio in her room and listened to a popular Chicago DJ almost nightly when she was a teenager.

My grandmother Deda and Mr. Hurd had a set in their home in Mt. Pleasant. Deda loved *"I Love Lucy,"* as did millions of other Americans. It was only years later I realized that show introduced something new to America: a family with a Hispanic male lead, Desi Arnaz as Ricky Ricardo.

Now in the late 1960s, I was making part of my living writing and producing radio and television commercials. I actually worked with some local talent whom I had heard on the air growing up in Paris a few years before. One announcer in particular became a good friend—Jack. I was a frequent guest in his home. His wife had two lovely daughters about my age!

One of the few pieces of furniture I owned was a second-hand piano I had purchased after moving to the upstairs apartment. I wrote a silly song—words and music—called "Xanadu." I played it for Jack. He got excited and asked if he could pitch it to a friend in the music business. If it sold, Jack would get a 10 percent agent's fee. It was a standard business arrangement, I was told.

We met at the publisher's offices on Music Row. I had recorded a crude "demo" on the piano. Despite its poor quality, both Jack and his music buddy liked the lyrics. They never said much about the music.

I signed a one-year contract on my song. A studio demo was cut using a rock band from out of state looking for their first hit. They would have to keep on looking.

The song was never picked up by anyone. After a year elapsed, so did the contract and the song became mine once again!

In October, 1967 I turned twenty-two. I had made it, or so I thought! I was single, making a good living doing something I liked! I should have been grateful to the Lord. But during my college years, I had quit going to church.

I never stopped believing in the Lord, but did move further away from my relationship with Him. Because I was now a young man, I suppose I thought I had outgrown Him! Time would show how wrong I was!

It was about this time I received a phone call for Coach Ben Jobe. It was Sunday afternoon and I was at home when the phone rang. I answered and heard a voice say, "Is this Ben Jobe, the basketball coach at Talladega?"

I was mystified, but answered, "No, this is Ben Jobe, the copywriter in Nashville!" The caller apologized and hung up.

I did not think about this until several years later when the same thing happened again. In fact, it kept on happening again and again! Over time, I became fascinated with this other Ben Jobe and wanted to meet him. Finally, in April, 2008, I did, some four decades after the first phone call. The life threads of two Ben Jobes were finally joined!

Mr. Cool

My advertising career was going well and I was making enough money that I decided to become more "hip" in my attire. It was 1968 and the hippie counterculture had influenced a lot of things, including clothing. I had always been a conservative dresser. Dressing up meant a white shirt and tie from Howard & Jobe. Now that look was old hat, at least to many in my generation.

One spring day after I had gotten paid, I went to a large downtown department store and bought some turtleneck tops in several colors. I began wearing them to work. No one seemed to mind. Some ad people I knew prided themselves on being "with it" and "hip"—more than the general population.

To add to my new look, I even bought a "Nehru" suit. This had been inspired by Jawaharlal Nehru (1889–1964), India's first prime minister. The West was looking East in the late '60s, partly due to the Beatles. They had spent time in India with a "maharishi." The Beatles included sitars on their albums. This Indian instrument became widely used in popular music of all kinds.

Many young men also sported longer hair and beards. The hit musical on Broadway that year was *"Hair."* I decide to grow some of my own. An art director at our agency made suggestions about what kind of facial hair. He drew a sketch of my face with various styles. I settled on a goatee and mustache with hair down to my collar.

I did not tell my family about this. Mom and Marilyn came to Nashville on a visit a few weeks after the facial hair had become part of my face. They stopped by my office late one afternoon. Marilyn came in, leaving Mom in the car. She was surprised, but her overriding emotion was fear about Mom's reaction!

My sister rushed out to the parking lot ahead of me to warn Mom. She was not thrilled, to say the least. The next time I visited Paris, I went to church with my folks. After the service, a man stopped me whose daughter I had known in high school. He pointed to my face and asked, incredulously, "Ben, what does all this mean?!"

I mumbled something about a "new look."

What *did* it mean? Now that I am a professor of speech communications, I realize the extra hair sent a strong nonverbal message. I don't have a clue what it meant! To complete my "fashion statement," on the same trip home I wore my Nehru suit into Howard & Jobe. Naturally, this surprised everyone.

Mom told me later, privately, it had embarrassed Dad. At the time I was so self-absorbed, I could not understand why a Nehru suit would do that. But, Howard & Jobe's men's department had sold tailored suits since before I was born. I might as well have publicly proclaimed these suits were not good enough for me anymore! My attempt to weave a "hip" thread had backfired!

More Madness

On April 4, 1968, a spring day quickly turned into a nightmare for millions of Americans of all races. Dr. Martin Luther, King, Jr., was in Memphis because of a garbage strike. Standing on the balcony of his motel, he was gunned down by an assassin! It was like Dallas all over again!

His body was flown back to Atlanta for the funeral, which was televised worldwide. Today, the Martin Luther King National Historical Site, operated by the US Department of the Interior, keeps his memory alive. King is buried there. On his tomb are the closing words of "I Have a Dream" (quoted from an old African-American spiritual) "Free at last! Free at last! Thank God Almighty, we are free at last!"

For several days after the King assassination, America was in shock once again. There was a real fear that King's sudden, violent death would provoke race rioting. On the weekend after his murder in Memphis, the Grand Ole Opry, which played at the Ryman Auditorium downtown, did not perform. There was a good reason: Nashville authorities had declared a curfew!

On October 14, 2011, some friends and I toured the National Civil Rights Museum, which was built on the site of the motel where King was gunned down. It was an overwhelming experience! We watched a powerful video about a man who was an eyewitness to the crime.

On June 6, 1968, in Los Angeles, shortly after being declared winner of the California Democratic Primary, presidential candidate Robert F. Kennedy, brother of the slain president, was himself assassinated in a hotel by a lone gunman named Sirhan Sirhan. Just two months after the King assassination, this latest bloodshed traumatized a nation already reeling from the shock of King's death.

The Democratic National Convention in Chicago later that summer featured live television coverage of police beating up antiwar demonstrators who chanted, "The whole world is watching!" Much of the world WAS watching on television, via satellites. So far, 1968 seemed to be a year like no other.

I remember a one-day business trip to Memphis that summer. The ad agency sent an art director and me to get some film processed for a television commercial. There was no such film lab in Nashville at the time. Our boss gave us his big air-conditioned car and a credit card to pay for gas and meals.

Interstate 40 was complete between the outskirts of Nashville and Memphis. We left about 6:00 a.m. and by 9:30 were dropping off the film at the lab. They told us it would be ready about 3:00 p.m. We had the rest of the day free, as long as we picked up the film on time.

After hanging out at the zoo in Overton Park, my art director friend suggested we eat lunch downtown and stay there until it was time to pick up the film. We parked the car nearby and walked down Front Street—so called because it is near the Mississippi River. There we saw striking garbage workers—all black men—carrying the same signs that had been televised all over the nation after King's assassination a few months earlier.

They read: "I AM a Man" The signs said nothing about higher wages, better working conditions, or anything else, just "I AM a Man"! Sometimes *simple* gets the job done better than *complicated*. "I AM a Man" summed up what millions of black men deserved—to be treated as persons made in the image of God!

We picked up our film at 3:00 p.m. and drove back to Nashville. But seeing those signs had dampened my enthusiasm for the trip. The ugly thread of racism seemed to reach out like tentacles to strangle us all!

Music City Ups and Downs

Not all the summer of 1968 was depressing. Bob Dylan had recorded his *"Nashville Skyline"* album here. I knew the photographer who took the cover photos; he also did a lot of work for our ad agency. Dylan's good friend Johnny Cash had a network television show on ABC, which was taped at the Ryman Auditorium—home of the Grand Old Opry.

Tickets to the taping of each show were free! I remember waiting in a line that stretched around the corner of Fifth Avenue for over an hour to get my free ticket with thousands of others. We packed the place.

Finally, Johnny Cash introduced his friend Bob Dylan. The crowd cheered for a long time. When we finally quieted down, Dylan sang and Cash sang and everyone in the audience loved it! That's one reason why they call Nashville Music City, USA!

I had written a radio spot for our meat-packing client, which proved to be a local hit. The radio stations played it for weeks. People even called in to request this commercial, if you can believe that. One of the listeners was the creative director from the big ad agency in the L & C Tower, at the time the largest agency in Tennessee.

He called and asked me to come to their place for an interview. I was offered a job as a copywriter on the basis of that single radio spot, plus my print samples, which I had learned to keep updated and ready to show.

I gave my notice and moved to an office in the tallest building in Nashville. This was around the time I turned twenty-three in the fall of 1968. My salary was 50 percent larger than what it had been at the old agency. I continued to live in the same modest furnished apartment, but reasoned that I had been driving the same car since 1965, so it was time for new one.

I did not know anything about buying a vehicle then and I'm sure I did not get the best deal I could get. But I traded in the old Chevy for a brand-new Mercury Cougar two-door sedan. It was black and gold, with black upholstery and bucket seats. The car had air-conditioning and automatic transmission like the Chevy. (I later learned to drive a stick shift, but back then I did not know how.)

What I remember about this car is how much fun it was to drive and how much the payments were: steep enough that I really needed to keep my cheap apartment!

Now I was working for the largest agency in my native state, in the tallest building in Nashville. I was only twenty-three and I honestly believe this all went to my head. I had arrived! (Not sure where, but time would tell.)

I wrote a campaign for a local bank for Christmas. In those days, banks had "Christmas Clubs" that offered savings accounts for the holidays. My brainchild was a "disease" you supposedly got if you did not join their Christmas Club: YULEOPHOBIA!

The Yuleophobia campaign became another local hit. There were newspaper ads and a radio spot. The agency president sent out a memo congratulating me! I had been there for only a few months!

An opportunity also came to write music for a television commercial. Another copywriter created this campaign. I wrote the music and the agency hired a talented man from the music industry to produce it in the studio.

The commercial ran in several states for a long time.

At this point, I was naive about office protocol. I knew a little about how songwriters made their living through fees paid by the users of their music. I had written the commercial's music for the simple joy of getting it heard on the air. I never expected any payment.

However, after the commercial aired, the account executive approached me one day and told me they had some money left in the production budget. He suggested I request a modest payment: $300. This seemed fair enough.

I asked for the money and the reaction was not at all what I expected. I received a check for $300. But two weeks later, I was fired! My creative director told me it was because I did not go through the proper channels to ask for payment. He said I should have asked him first! (I didn't know.)

It was the first time I had ever lost a job. I went back to the old agency where I had started a year and a half before. They gave me some steady work but in a freelance capacity. I stayed there for several months while deciding what to do.

To save on expenses, I moved out of my upstairs apartment off West End into a two-bedroom, two-bath apartment in a complex one block off Eighth Avenue South, not far from Music Row. My roommates were two former Peabody music majors, Richard Law and Randy Roman. (I am still close to Richard, as he and his wife, Mary, live in the same part of Nashville I do.). My share of the rent was $45 a month. I stayed there the rest of the year.

Even though my advertising career was not what it had been, the year 1969 had a lot of pleasant distractions. The summer featured two big events of the decade: the

Apollo moon landing and the rock music festival at Woodstock, New York. The moon landing featured a few astronauts who made history. Woodstock featured a cast of half a million hippies!

Watching the Apollo moon landing on television took me back to the fall of 1957 in Paris. The Russian unmanned satellite Sputnik could be seen crossing the night sky. The "space race" had added a new dimension to the Cold War. Rockets used for war could also be used to explore space.

I remember the attempted "launch" of a pet hamster in a homemade rocket by some of my Boy Scout friends on a cold New Year's Day a couple of years later. The animal survived the trip upward but seemed dazed by the experience. The "space trip" lasted less than a minute and we found the hamster inside its nose cone in a neighbor's yard. One of our own "rocket boys" ended up working for NASA.

Also in the summer of 1969, a friend and I went to Atlanta to an outdoor music festival—a sort of Southern "Woodstock." It was held at the Atlanta International Raceway south of the city. There must have been a couple of hundred thousand people there. I remember we occupied the same spot of ground, wedged in between many others for nineteen hours except for trips to the restroom!

One weekend that summer, my parents asked me to meet them in Smyrna to be part of a special event: the dedication of a roadside historical marker about DeWitt Smith Jobe, the Confederate hero in our family.

I attended the dedication and met my cousin John Moore for the first time. We saw the actual Jobe farmhouse—still occupied, but not by our family—on Rocky Fork Road outside Smyrna.

It was an important event in my life, though at the time I had no clue how important! Looking back, I see it was another time of threads coming together. But I had no clue where they would lead.

Atlanta's Siren Song

By the end of 1969, I had decided to try my luck in Atlanta, which offered more opportunities than Nashville. I moved my few things home, worked for Howard & Jobe through the holiday rush, then persuaded my parents to help me make the move.

I needed their help because I had lost my car. The Cougar would have been repossessed but for my announcer friend Jack, who bought it for his wife. My parents made me an offer I could not refuse: they would get me to Atlanta and provide me with a motel for one week.

If I could not get a job in that time, I would return to Paris and work in the store! After looking a few days, I found a copywriting job with an Atlanta ad agency.

I moved to Atlanta, found a nice one-bedroom apartment and bought a new Volkswagen Beetle, all in the next week. There was just one problem. I did not know how to drive the VW's stick shift. Dad gave me some brief lessons in the parking lot of my apartment before he returned to Paris.

I remember killing the VW's engine in traffic and stalling on an upgrade many times before I finally mastered the stick. But, I have driven only stick-shift vehicles ever since. I put over a hundred thousand miles on that Beetle, including having the engine rebuilt, before I finally traded it for a VW Rabbit in 1975.

The year 1970 was filled with several different agency jobs, but the only one I remember fondly was for an Atlanta branch of a New York agency that handled part of the Coca-Cola account. I was there two months in a free-lance capacity to fill in for another writer who had to have surgery. There were promises of a "possibility" of regular employment later.

But on a Friday in August, just before lunch, the entire staff was summoned to the conference room for an announcement. The New York headquarters had decided to move the account group closer to the main creative people there! Translation: they did not need the Atlanta office anymore. It would be closed!

I found another agency job soon after that, but the instability of this business had taken away the initial thrill I had felt back in Nashville. I became restless and distracted and my work showed it. I was fired from this new job after about two months.

Miraculously, I found yet another agency copywriting job after that. It would prove to be the final agency job in Atlanta and the doorway to a totally new career experience.

One day, a young man (younger than I was) came to see me at work. He was a self-employed jingle writer and producer. He played me his sample tape and I was impressed. I played him a tape of music I had written for commercials in Nashville, such as the one that had gotten me fired at the big agency.

The young man (whom I'll call Jeff) was surprised and seemed to like my work. We went out to lunch. Later, Jeff called and asked if I would write a jingle for him. He said we would split the profits fifty-fifty. I jumped at the chance to do music and make money at it.

This was about the time I was shown the door at the fourth and final Atlanta agency. My career as a copywriter in Big A had lasted only about sixteen months! But the prospect of writing jingles for a living beckoned like a distant pot of gold.

Jeff and I worked together for the next two years. We called our company Imagine, Ltd. The name came from the title of the John Lennon song. I got used to spending much time in the studio and writing jingles at home. (I still had my piano.)

Jeff was originally from Buffalo, New York, and of Italian ancestry. He was married and had a young son. Jeff's parents came once for a visit and I met them. His father was not too thrilled by our musical enterprise and asked me to talk his son out of it! No way!

Jeff did the sales work and produced the music. His father made a living as a salesman. Jeff followed in his footsteps and got us some good clients. We created music for the Atlanta regional Sears stores, a large pest-control company, and several banks. I was the company's in-house writer and arranger. Jeff kept busy drumming up clients and producing in the studio. I joined him in the studio and learned a lot about this phase of the business.

Our biggest-name jobs were television themes for the Atlanta Hawks (NBA) and the Braves baseball team. The Braves theme ran on a regional network all across the South and was still running years later when I had left Atlanta for graduate school in Kentucky.

You might think we both became wealthy from these jobs—especially the Braves theme. Wrong! Getting these jobs brought in more work, but as time went on, personal differences between the two partners became serious. Jeff and I had a complete falling out and parted company late in 1973.

Eventually, he and his family moved to New York City where he became very successful in commercial music. "Jeff," if you are reading this, thanks for the opportunity to make music together. I wish you all the best!

I decided to go free-lance as a jingle writer after our split. Had this been Nashville, it might have worked. But Atlanta is not Music City! I spent most of the year living hand to mouth. Jeff hired me to write and arrange a few jobs for him. But my overall direction was downhill.

There had been some bright spots during my Atlanta years: dates, concerts, plays, and scenic weekend trips to the North Georgia mountains with an attractive female neighbor who was a graphic artist. We dated for a while. There were other women in my life besides her but I remember the artist best of all. She lived right around the corner.

Marilyn and Jack came to Atlanta in summer, 1974. The three of us crowded into my VW Beetle as we headed to a Braves game to see Hank Aaron play. Marilyn was pregnant with Heather, who was born the following January, so I do not know how the VW held us all, but it did! I visited them in Easley from time to time.

The fall of 1974 was the moment of truth. I had never really made much money with the jingle company. I had played piano in some cocktail lounges and restaurants (much to my parents' dismay) and this continued to be a source of income. But it was not enough to live on.

I reluctantly returned to Paris around Thanksgiving to work for Howard & Jobe. I told myself I would help the family business out through the Christmas rush, then return to Atlanta one more time. In reality, I was the one who needed help!

Returning to Atlanta in January, I quickly realized my time there was at an end. Not knowing what the future held, I was grateful I had a family to go home to. I was twenty-nine years old with long hair and a full beard. Mom and Dad were not ready for a son-turned-hippie back at home. Neither was I!

My attempt to weave my life on my own had not been as successful as I had hoped. The next thread would mean going back to my roots: Paris, Tennessee.

Big Changes

It was a difficult time for all three of us. Mom and Dad were living in the renovated two-bedroom apartment in downtown Paris that would be their last home before moving to Vero Beach, Florida, in 1979. I slept on the fold-out sofa bed in the living room.

I worked for Howard & Jobe and returned to First Baptist Church. I was welcomed back at church but privately felt like the Prodigal Son returning from the faraway country. I had slipped into some lifestyle patterns in Atlanta that were literally far from what I had been taught in church and at home.

The way back to church had been paved with a book I had bought while in Atlanta—*The Late, Great Planet Earth* by Hal Lindsey. It was eventually named the best-selling book of the entire decade of the 1970s by the *New York Times*.

The Late, Great Planet Earth connected current events with the soon return Jesus Christ. I had been in church since I was a baby but this was all new to me! Lindsey's book gave me a desire to know the Lord better since He could return at any moment. It also fueled an interest in Bible prophecy that continues today—the prophecy thread!

Paris of my childhood and Paris in the 1970s seemed to be the same. But I was rudely reminded one day of how the place was changing. New people were moving into the area. Not all of them were a civic improvement!

I went into a barbershop for a haircut and sat down in the chair. The barber began cutting my hair. After several moments of silence, I spoke to him.

"Where are you from, sir?" I asked.

"Detroit," he said in a noticeable Midwestern accent.

"Why did you move here?"

His reply cracked like a whiplash across my face:

"To get away from the niggers!"

I do not remember what I said in reply, but after I had paid him, I left that barbershop, vowing never to return. This had happened a few times before—a Northern transplant assumed that because I am a white Southerner, I am as racist as him! That really made me mad!

I had never really given much thought about the next phase of my life. What's next? What would I do? What *could* I do?! My parents never insisted I take over the store. Mom told me years later they always believed Howard & Jobe was not part of my destiny. They were right!

Then one day I saw Miss Ruby Krider. She stopped in the middle of the sidewalk to chat. Miss Ruby asked how I was and what my plans were. Then she came right to the point.

"Ben, I'm teaching at Murray State (in Murray, Kentucky, twenty-four miles north). In fact, I'll be teaching a college class here at the high school in creative dramatics starting in January. Why don't you sign up for it?"

It seemed like a good idea. I took the class, which met one night a week at Henry County High School. Miss Ruby was in her seventies, but was still a fine teacher. I enjoyed the class and meeting the other students. Many were newcomers to Paris—and none seemed like that redneck barber from Detroit!

The Murray State class at the high school led to two more classes in the summer of 1975 at the main campus in Murray, Kentucky. One of these was in video production. For my project, I created a tribute to Grove High School, which was now history thanks to the new consolidated Henry County High. I called it *"The School That Came from a Bottle."*

I took 35-millimeter slides with a borrowed camera, wrote the narration, and recorded it along with music I had composed. I recorded the music in a small studio in rural Henry County called The Sound Farm. The narration was recorded at a Paris radio station. One of the announcers, Bill McCutcheon, was a friend from Grove

High days and took a personal interest in my project. However, I voiced the narration myself.

I received an A for my work. The next year I was asked to show the Grove program to some Paris school and civic groups. (I still had the slides and soundtrack even though the university retained ownership of the videotape.) *"The School That Came from a Bottle"* was very well received—-better than a bottle of tasteless chill tonic!

That fall of 1975, I rented a room in the Phi Mu Alpha house near the Murray State campus. I stayed there during the week. My classes met Tuesday through Friday morning. I worked at Howard & Jobe from noon to 8:00 p.m. on Friday, all day Saturday and Monday. I would return to Murray on Monday evening for another week at school.

Miss Ruby had helped me get a partial teaching assistantship and I taught one undergraduate speech class to earn my keep. I enjoyed teaching and still do. I was a graduate assistant in communications. I shared an office with another graduate student.

The 1970 VW Beetle had over a hundred thousand miles. I traded it that summer for a new VW Rabbit. My assistantship was just enough to cover the payments. I began to date an undergraduate student I had met during the Christmas holidays at church. She went to Murray State, but her family lived in Paris and knew mine.

The year 1976 was our nation's Bicentennial. It was also when I finished my studies and received my master's degree in speech communication.

In June that year, something happened that showed me in no uncertain terms the next step in my journey. The young woman I was dating and I had gone with our church's youth choir to a Southern Baptist summer conference center at Ridgecrest, North Carolina, for a week of church music activities.

On the last night of the conference they gave an altar call for those who wanted to surrender themselves to the Lord for ministry. I felt a tug in my spirit, as if I were supposed to respond. But, I did not go forward.

That night, I had a strange, frightening dream. I woke up and prayed, asking God to forgive my inaction the previous evening. I vowed to do the right thing at the next opportunity. The following Sunday at First Baptist Church in Paris, I gave my life to ministry in the presence of my home church family.

I had been miserable during the last few months in Atlanta in 1974. I now believe this discomfort was caused by the Lord calling me, even as I had heard His Voice calling me when I was a child. But this time, His call was for me to give myself and my music back to Him. Finally, in 1976, I obeyed!

I graduated from Murray State in August and continued to work at Howard & Jobe until January, 1977. I had been accepted as a student at The Southern Baptist

Theological Seminary in Louisville, Kentucky. I would major in church music. Finally, it was time to leave home.

I drove to Louisville on a cold, snowy day in late January to enter seminary. My VW Rabbit was loaded with personal items for my dorm room on campus. I moved in and began to prepare for classes.

I soon became part of a huge media event. It seemed almost everyone on campus was watching the television mini-series *"Roots."* I had a copy of the book, which had come out the previous year. Like most eyes in the nation, mine were glued to the television set for a week as this epic story unfolded. The mini-series was seen by 130 million people.

The author, Alex Haley (1921–1992), was a Tennessean who used oral history in his own family to trace his African ancestry back to Kunta Kinte, who had been captured and brought to America as a slave in 1767! Haley's tale of his family's survival against overwhelming odds brought him worldwide recognition and a Pulitzer Prize. "Roots" captured the imagination of America and the world.

I began attending classes and taking piano lessons again. Because I had not finished my undergraduate music major at Peabody (changing majors twice), I was required to take undergraduate courses to make up for this deficiency before beginning the master's program in church music. It was a long, grueling process, but

I stuck it out. I wanted that graduate music degree! I majored in piano and composition.

Southern Seminary was home for nearly four years. I graduated in December, 1980. I was thirty-five years old. I had entered as a single man and departed four years later as a husband and father. I had married the young woman (whom I'll call Leanne) from Paris on July 16, 1977. Our son, Joshua, was born March 21, 1980. I was there for the big event.

Mom and Dad, by this time, were living in Vero Beach, Florida. They made the long drive to Louisville in spring, 1980, to see their only Jobe grandchild. By the end of the year when I graduated, they were living on Camille Street in Easley, South Carolina, so the trip was much shorter.

Leanne had worked in the seminary music library most of our time at Southern. We lived on campus. I had several part-time jobs, including a brief one as a minister of music at a church.

Nashville beckoned and we began to plan how to get there. My goal was to work at the Baptist Sunday School Board, our denomination's publishing house.

In February, 1981, after three weeks with Leanne's parents in Paris, we moved to Nashville. Leanne found a job in the business office of a hospital. I finally got a job in June—as a copywriter in my former ad agency from 1968. We lived in a duplex in suburban Hermitage and found daycare for Josh nearby. Our Nashville thread had begun.

Part Five:

Tennessee Tapestry

"You shall love your neighbor as yourself"

(Leviticus 19:18).

When I was hired by my old ad agency in June, 1981, after an absence of nearly thirteen years, I was grateful to find a job doing something I liked. But my ultimate goal in Nashville was to work for the Baptist Sunday School Board, our denomination's large publishing house. For now, at least I had a job.

The old agency had changed since 1968. Two of the three partners had left, but the one remaining had kept all three names in the firm. This seemed strange, but I was so glad to have work I did not mind. I worked on mostly local accounts. A series of print ads I wrote for a men's apparel shop won an award from the local ad club, as did a radio spot for a car dealer.

The morning after I learned about this, I went to the office expecting a pat on the back. Instead, the secretary said, "Don't say anything to Mr. — about the award."

"Why not?" I asked.

"Because," she said, "he doesn't like the ad club. Your winning the awards means he has to go to the ad club banquet. He's mad about it!"

This was a red flag! Then over the next few months, our business began to taper off. There were days with nothing to do. Finally, in June of 1982, I was laid off for lack of work. I had been there for a year. Our parting was amicable.

I quickly found not one, but two jobs—working part-time two days a week each at two different agencies. This free-lance arrangement kept food on the table. Eventually, I found a regular full-time job with a third agency.

All this time, I kept trying to get my foot in the door at the Sunday School Board. I filled out an application and left it with their personnel department, but nothing happened.

By this time, Leanne and I had joined First Baptist Church in downtown Nashville. It was within walking distance of the Sunday School Board. A number of employees, department heads and even the president of the Board were church members!

A young man I knew in the choir worked at the Board. He was interested in my copywriting, as he had to do this himself at work. He hired me to write some ads for him free-lance. One day in the summer of 1983, I was taking what I had written to his office at the Board.

A familiar face appeared in the door of the personnel department. It belonged to a former seminary student I had known in Louisville.

"Ben," he said. "Stop by here before you leave. I have something that might interest you!"

When I stopped by personnel, my friend showed me a job posting for a copy editor at Broadman Press, the Board's non-denominational book publisher. I filled out another application and it was sent on its way.

I soon heard from Broadman. I went for an interview and was offered a temporary spot in the copy editor position. If I "worked out," it would be more than temporary.

I reported for my first day on the job September 7, 1983. Ironically, this was my parents' and my sister's and brother-in-law's wedding anniversaries!

For me, it would be the beginning of a fascinating corporate relationship that would last a decade!

I was "baptized" in books—manuscripts, proofs, and so forth. I was part of the editorial team, working closely with other editors. Some of these editors were ordained ministers, but there were some women, including one who had been promoted from copy editor.

There were two other copy editors, both women. I was the lone male copy editor.

On October 1, I was offered the job full time. I officially became part of the Broadman Products Department—books and music section. They said I was a "good fit" because I had both editorial skills and the music degree. This helped get me the job since they also published books on music.

The Baptist Sunday School Board was a whole world unto itself. It had been founded in 1891 and, by the time I became an employee in 1983, had well over a thousand employees. Their property covered several blocks of downtown Nashville and was over a million square feet! Everything about the place was overwhelming and fascinating at the same time.

By this time, our family was living in a townhouse apartment in Franklin, about twenty miles south of Nashville. Josh was in daycare there and Leanne worked for Belmont University's library in Nashville, where she also took classes toward finishing her degree. She eventually graduated from Belmont. The next thread caught me completely by surprise!

Family Destruction

Leanne had suffered with depression ever since I had known her. In 1984, after I had been at the Board less than a year, she had a nervous breakdown. She was unable to work and began seeing a female counselor.

It was another red flag, but I was so absorbed by my work I did not notice.

Despite finally getting my dream job, I still had anger issues and was sometimes hard to live with. I have struggled with anger all of my life.

One day in 1985, Leanne came home from her session with the counselor and said, "—says we should get a divorce!"

It was like a nuclear bomb had dropped right on top of me! I will spare you some of the details, but those who have experienced divorce must know how terrible it can be! Looking back, I believe it was hardest on

Josh, who was only five! (He was six when the divorce became final.)

We moved into separate apartments in early 1986, on opposite sides of Franklin. Since we lived in Williamson County, we learned we would not have to go to court since we were agreed on the division of our property.

We had bought a house by then, but most of our "property" were debts! We simply divided them! We lost the house, in lieu of foreclosure. The marriage, on paper at least, had lasted nine years!

Our divorce became final in October, 1986, the month I turned forty-one. Josh was just six- and- a- half years old and in the first grade. I paid child support during the school year and kept Josh with me each summer. I had him for every other weekend. I paid the last child-support payment in June, 1998, after Josh had graduated from high school.

I was devastated at losing my family. I plunged into my work even more, which was easy because it was very demanding and extremely interesting. During the same year my wife and I divorced, there were two other divorces in our couples Sunday School class at church. Both men also worked at the Sunday School Board. One of these was the man in personnel whom I had known at seminary!

The reaction of my coworkers at the Board was varied. What was really unnerving was the number of total strangers who also worked there but who I did not know, who came to me "out of the woodwork" asking all about my divorce. I soon learned this part of my life was not private at all!

This all reminded me of growing up in Paris: living in a "fishbowl." I like blending into the crowd. I was counseled to do the same at the Baptist Sunday School Board by friends who had also been through a divorce while working there. I heeded their advice. My divorce thread was painful, but I tried to make the best of it.

Divine Sunshine

In the middle of this storm, a ray of divine sunshine pierced the darkness. Through a connection via my editor friend Joe Johnson, I was interviewed for a special free-lance job—composing music for two thirty-minute video productions. I still had the tapes from my Atlanta jingle-writing days and used them in the interview. Those jingle tapes helped me get this job!

When I had written that fanfare for the Grove Band in Paris back in 1962, I had adolescent dreams of someday going to Hollywood and writing movie scores. Instead, some twenty-four years later in 1986—on the heels of a divorce—I was writing music for two dramatic video productions at the Baptist Sunday School Board. The Board had a small recording studio where I recorded the music. It was all a blessing from the Lord!

Thankfully, working on Broadman books was a pleasant distraction from the pain of divorce and losing custody of my son. I stayed in this job for over nine years. I worked on books of all kinds—sermons and theology, church growth and administration, novels and poetry, music, biographies of pastors and missionaries. Broadman even published a series of "clean" joke books!

I became friends with some of my coworkers. One editor in particular, Joe Johnson (1933–2008), was special. Joe and I worked together on many projects during this nine-year period. A native of Knoxville, Tennessee, Joe had graduated from Mississippi College and New Orleans Baptist Theological Seminary. He had been a pastor in Mississippi during the civil- rights era.

Joe was also a music lover and sang very well—sometimes when others were trying to work! His "music library" included hymns and gospel songs, country, rock, Tin Pan Alley, and grand opera. Joe was a colorful character and a gifted editor as well. I loved him like a brother.

Another editor there with whom I am still close is Dr. Steve Bond. Steve's doctorate is in philosophy from Vanderbilt. He is a year older than I and was hired in 1976. As of 2012, he is still there—an editor in the Bible section of Broadman & Holman Publishers, the corporate successor to Broadman Press and the Holman Bible Division.

Broadman also published books for "special markets," including African-Americans. Joe was the editor for most of these "black books." I especially enjoyed working on these books because they had a lot of new information—at least to me!

For example, Noah's grandson Cush was probably a black man. He was the namesake of an ancient African kingdom whose inhabitants were called "Cushites." The word "Cushite" in the Old Testament always refers to an African. They never taught me about "Cushites" in my hometown church.

One benefit of this job was getting paid to read the Bible! I grew in my knowledge of Scripture. As I did, I became even more aware that racism, anti-Semitism, and sexism have no place in a Christian's life!

Paul wrote in his letter to the Galatians: "There is neither Jew nor Greek, there is neither slave nor free, there is neither male nor female; for you are all one in Christ Jesus" (3:28). The human family is a tapestry of many different colors, genders, nations, and faiths. Diversity is not "politically correct." It is biblically correct!

Such insights sparked intellectual and spiritual growth in my own life: an expanded worldview to include all the human race. This was a far cry from the racist nonverbal messages some people in Paris, Tennessee, had sent when I came of age during the end of the "Jim Crow" segregation era.

By 1987, I had adjusted to being a single parent. The routine of work and church were brightened by weekend visits by my young son, Josh. He was seven now and in the second grade. For his seventh birthday on

March 21, I hosted a birthday party for my son and the children of some of my Board coworkers. A couple of the kids' parents were Hispanic.

One of these Latin women was a native of San Antonio, Texas, of Mexican ancestry and a single parent. She had a daughter about Josh's age. From time to time, my work friend and I would get together with some other Board employees' kids so our two could play with other children.

My Latina friend asked if Josh could be in a photo shoot for the cover of a book for children's choir directors. Her daughter was to be in the shoot along with one other child. I asked Josh and he gladly agreed to participate. I still have a copy of the book with him and the two other kids on the cover.

About this time I met Esperanza (not her real name) and her mother.

These two lovely women were in their twenties and forties, respectively. Both were from Guatemala, but were active members of the Hispanic Baptist Mission at First Baptist Church. Esperanza was a singer and we met through a mutual friend. I became her "pianista"—accompanist.

Esperanza asked me to play for her whenever she sang a special at the mission, which met in the First Baptist complex. She and I became friends but she let it be known that was to be the extent of our relationship.

She and her mother were both single! The parents had divorced back in Guatemala.

However, she and her mother allowed Josh and me to be a part of their lives for a season. Esperanza and I kept busy rehearsing. Once in a while, the mission folks asked me to play a solo at the mission, even though they had a fine "pianista" of their own. The mission used a hymnbook published in El Paso, Texas, for Spanish-speaking Baptist churches throughout the United States and Latin America.

This collaboration between the Latina singer and me foreshadowed the next big thread: a mission trip to South America.

South of the Border

Sometimes I wondered why these two lovely Latin women had come into my life. In the spring of 1988, I had my answer. The Tennessee Baptist Convention announced a volunteer mission trip to Venezuela! I had worked with Esperanza for over a year. The mission trip would take my "south of the border" music to the next level.

I prayed about how to go to Venezuela. My finances were tight just making ends meet and paying child support. In answer to my prayers, the Lord provided. Funding came from the missions committee of my church, my parents, and from a small mission church in Thompson Station (south of Franklin, near Spring Hill) where I served as music director.

I got my passport and arranged to be off from the mission church for the two Sundays I would be gone. I planned to take all my annual vacation days from the

Sunday School Board. In fact, the Broadman Products Department gave me a surprise going-away party a few days before I left.

The trip to Venezuela was difficult for my eight-year-old son. Josh told me more than once, "I don't want you to go!" I explained over and over I would only be gone less than two weeks. Still, he was not happy.

By this time I was living in a new apartment complex across Franklin near Interstate 65, my route to downtown Nashville and the Board. Curiously, Leanne had also moved into the same complex, to a different building, but we were still "neighbors."

Josh would be in the third grade that fall, and school would start while I was away. My parents volunteered to stay in my apartment while I was in Venezuela, to "house sit" and see their grandson. My ex-wife was still on speaking terms with them so it all worked out. Mom and Dad got to spend some time with Josh and this seemed to make him feel better.

On the morning of our departure from the Nashville Airport, we boarded a flight to Atlanta. Our group changed planes there and went on to Miami, where we changed again from Delta Airlines to VIASA, the Venezuelan national airline.

Our plane was a wide-bodied 747 and held hundreds of passengers, including some 250 mission volunteers from across Tennessee. The flight took between three and four hours from Miami. We landed at Simon

Bolivar International Airport in the early evening, but it was still daylight.

Caracas's Airport, named for the country's "liberator," Simon Bolivar (1783–1830), was right by the ocean. Seawalls protected the runways from surging tides. We were met by a van that took us into the city.

The trip was only about thirty miles, but they were some of the most dramatic miles I have ever traveled. Our van wound upward through two long tunnels on an multi-lane expressway thick with traffic. When we cleared the end of the second tunnel, there was Caracas teeming with millions of people!

The huge, modern metropolis spread out across a broad mountain valley about three thousand feet above sea level. Lush green hills rose even higher on the sides of the valley. The van finally descended into the bustling urban sprawl and the effect was invigorating.

I fell in love with this city, its people and the country as well. The days we spent there will always be a part of me! Our group stayed in the Hilton Hotel downtown, across the street from an ultramodern performing arts center. We rode the subway, so new it was still under construction, to the church across town.

We boarded El Metro at Belles Artes (Fine Arts) station and rode to Gato Negro (Black Cat) station. The fare was relatively cheap: three B's (bolivars), about ten American cents at the time. Simon Bolivar is celebrated across Venezuela as the founding father of the nation. His name is everywhere, even on their money!

Our church was Iglesia Bautista Bethel, Bethel Baptist Church. It was in a working-class neighborhood about three blocks from the subway station. My group included two elderly ladies and myself. I had been appointed their "team leader."

On Sunday morning, after we arrived at the church, they told me I would be playing the piano AND preaching! They said the "team leader" always did the preaching!

I had brought my Bible, but this was a complete surprise. I had never preached before, either in English or Spanish! The church had a young seminary student who was bilingual; he became my interpreter.

Before leaving Nashville, some friends at the Board had given me a beginning Spanish-English primer. I struggled to make sense of it, but three years of Latin at Grove High School helped. Latin and Spanish are very close linguistically.

I tried to converse in Spanish. Most attempts ended badly because I could rarely finish the sentence I had started! But the Lord sent me an angel of mercy. She introduced herself, in very good English, after the Sunday morning service.

My "angel" was a nursing student twenty-two years old who had lived in the United States a few years before. She became my interpreter, tour guide, and helper.

I was a divorced man almost forty-three, but that did not seem to matter. This lovely Latin "angel" was my *amiga* (friend) for the week!

To keep up appearances, my "angel" suggested I allow her to take along her female friend, who was married to a seminary student. We three spent our days taking in Caracas, while we visited people in the "Black Cat" neighborhood and invited them to church. The church held services each night and several people we invited came.

I remember their singing, how powerful and heartfelt! My preaching was OK, I guess, but I believe part of its appeal was simply that we were visiting Americans! When we were there in 1988, Venezuela was extremely pro-American. Many of the people at church would tell me they had a brother in Oklahoma City, a son in Miami, or had been to Walt Disney World in Florida.

Later, when I got back home, I looked on a map and realized from Nashville to Miami is about one-third of the way from Nashville to Caracas! Flying from Miami to Venezuela, perched on the northern tip of South America, is only about two-thirds of the trip!

Our week in Venezuela's capital city flew by. The next Sunday was our last. The weeklong series of services finally ended. We said our good-byes and my Latin "angel" gave me a big hug! She seemed sad to see me go! I remember feeling the same way about her!

On Monday morning, our group boarded another van to ride back to the airport and begin the flight back home. Our return flight was uneventful. I remember everyone on the plane cheered loudly when the wheels of the VIASA 747 touched the Miami runway. Back on American soil at last!

After a layover in Miami, we flew Delta back to Atlanta, changed planes for the last time, and returned to Nashville. My parents met me at the airport. The next day they drove back to Easley, South Carolina, and I went in to work. I remember feeling very tired and not getting much done that day, but I had enough memories from Venezuela to last a lifetime: a beautiful Latin thread from south of the border.

There's one other place in the world I want to go before I die: Israel. My mother went in 1982 and someone else I know went in 2008. I want to go there myself. It would be amazing to be in the Holy Land where Jesus walked, taught, performed miracles, died, and rose again! Israel: where the threads of Bible stories I had learned since childhood were all woven together.

Love Song

The late 1980s had some other bright spots besides the Venezuela trip. In 1987, an art director I knew at the Board asked me to help her write a song for her own wedding later that year. It was to be a surprise for her fiancé.

My art director friend Marcy had written some lyrics. I got busy and wrote a melody for them. Marcy really liked what I had written. She and her fiancé knew some people at their church in the contemporary Christian music business. Marcy rounded some of them up and we made a demo at a home studio. The studio owner refused to charge us for it, calling it a wedding present for Marcy and her fiancé, Mark.

Later that summer, "The Mystery of Love," was unveiled for the first time at their wedding. Someone came up and complimented Marcy afterward. I was standing nearby and she turned and introduced us. The man worked for a well-known producer who specialized in contemporary Christian music!

After Marcy and Mark returned from their honeymoon, she went back to her job at the Board. One day, she called and said she knew someone at a major Christian publisher who would listen to our demo. She asked my permission.

I agreed!

Our demo made its way through the giant music-publishing company. Finally, we heard they were going to publish "The Mystery of Love" in an album of wedding songs! Not long after that, a man called me to confirm this. He asked me to could come by his office and sign a contract. This time, it was not a one-year contract like my silly '60s song "Xanadu."

A top arranger in Christian music orchestrated our song. In due course, the song was recorded and released on the wedding album. I still have copies of it even though the song has been out of print for a long time.

Years later, I would tell this story and then dramatically finish with: "And I have made HUNDREDS of dollars from it!" usually with a chuckle!

I used the song in my own wedding on August 20, 1991. I had met the new Mrs. Ben Jobe at Rayon City Baptist Church in Old Hickory when I went there as staff pianist in April. It was strange playing the piano in my own wedding, but somehow I managed it!

My best man was a close friend Joe Johnson had introduced me to back in 1985. Zander Dell Raines worked at the Sunday School Board 28 years and retired in July, 2008. He and his wife have three grown children, and several grandchildren. They all live in Lebanon, east of Nashville, and we still see each other often.

Dell Raines is a man of many talents. He is also a volunteer with our denomination's North American Mission Board and works closely with the Hispanic Baptist Missions in Lebanon and Carthage. In the early 1970s, he played bass in a gospel group and was their only white member! He is one of several good friends I made while working at the Board.

In the early 1990s a coworker gave me a photocopy of a magazine article called "The Trials of Jobe." It was about Coach Ben. The person who gave me the article made a joke of it, saying, "Here's your long-lost brother!"

I was intrigued once more with this prominent black basketball coach. The article fueled my fascination. It said Coach Ben was originally from Nashville, Tennessee, and had graduated from Fisk University! I filed it away for future reference but my curiosity was kindled after numerous phone calls for him ever since the late 1960s. I wondered if we would ever meet.

In 1991, the same year I got married again, a new administration took over at the Sunday School Board. The new leadership began making major changes in the century-old organization. The biggest was a complete restructuring and downsizing.

This hit like an earthquake! In 1992–93, hundreds of longtime employees were given a choice of taking a retirement package or losing their jobs. Eligibility for the package was based on a formula: age plus years of service. Some who were not eligible to retire like me were given new assignments. I found a position in another department.

Joe Johnson, my dear friend at Broadman, was one of many who reluctantly took the retirement "package." The alternative was not having a job. Even our department head was among the new retirees. The bosses cleaned house!

In late September, 1993, after a few months into my new job, I was asked one Tuesday to report to Human Resources. They gave me a ten-year service award. On Thursday, my boss told me to go to HR again.

My position had been deleted in the ongoing downsizing! I was given four months' severance pay. It was the end of a ten-year career and the beginning of another chapter in my life.

When I first went to work for the Board in 1983, a church friend had congratulated me: "Well, Ben, we heard you got on at the Board. Now, you'll have a job for the rest of your life!"

Lifetime employment at the denomination's giant publishing house became a thing of the past in the '90s.

Downsizing was not the only change. Even the corporate name itself was changed to Lifeway Christian Resources. So now you can work for Lifeway, but rarely for a lifetime!

The Lifeway thread was a time of growth, change, and friendship. Some of those friends remain very important threads in my Tennessee tapestry

Here Comes the Professor

For a few months after leaving Lifeway, I did free-lance editorial and marketing work but deep down I knew there was not much future in it. Free-lancing means only getting paid now and again. I needed something more dependable. So did those who depended on me.

By then it was 1994 and we were living in Gallatin. I took a job delivering pizza locally. But this did not cover all our expenses.

Gallatin is home to Volunteer State Community College. Joe Johnson and Dr. Steve Bond, my good friends from Broadman days, had both urged me to consider college teaching. They said I would be good at it! I was also encouraged by my cousin Bill, a retired educator.

I applied at Volunteer State and waited. For months I did not hear anything and considered it a lost cause. Finally, one hot July day, a letter came requesting my presence at their annual adjunct faculty in-service training.

I was excited and dumbfounded at the same time! This was the first communication I had received from the college since I had applied in December, 1993. I called the office on campus that sent the letter. The woman I spoke with said, "Well, if they weren't planning on using you to teach, they wouldn't have sent the letter!"

The next step in my journey was finally clear: college professor! I had two graduate degrees. What better way to use them than teaching college students? Mom also gave her blessing. She said I would be a "natural."

In late August, a week before fall classes began, I attended the adjunct in-service event. There I met for the first time my boss and mentor Virginia Thigpen. Ginny apologized for not getting in touch with me earlier. She gave me a single speech class that met once a week, on Wednesday evenings. This would be a trial run, so to speak.

I continued to deliver pizza on weekends and taught the class on Wednesday evenings. Today, after teaching thousands of students at several area colleges, I realize how patient Vol State must have been with me. That first semester, I was the "blind leading the blind." But slowly, after much hard work, I developed a workable vision of how to teach.

In the spring of 1995, I taught more speech classes at Vol State. Then, Ginny asked if I would also like to teach that fall at Middle Tennessee State University in Murfreesboro. They needed help with public speaking classes on Monday, Wednesday, and Friday. Ginny suggested some Tuesday–-Thursday classes at Vol State so I could also teach at MTSU.

I made the long drive to Murfreesboro from Gallatin, about forty-five miles, and met with their department chair. I was assigned three classes on Monday, Wednesday, and Friday to start in late August with the fall term.

During the summer of 1995, I taught only one class for Vol State and worked extra hours at the pizza place. Summers have always been on the lean side, as there are not many classes available but the fall and spring semesters more than make up for it. In recent years, my summers have become busier. (In the summer of 2012, I taught three classes.)

In July, 1995, Mom died after a losing battle with complications from cancer surgery. She was seventy-six. Dad moved into assisted living the next year.

That fall, I also began teaching a class in music appreciation at Vol State. A year after beginning my teaching career, I was using both of my graduate degrees! I had found my niche. I later realized many of my previous jobs and careers were necessary preparation for teaching.

For MTSU, I taught at their huge Murfreesboro campus. Sometimes they would schedule my classes in different buildings. I walked a lot and even ran to get to class on time. I needed the exercise but it was hectic.

Vol State has off-campus sites scattered across several counties in their vast Middle Tennessee service area. Besides the main campus in Gallatin, I also taught wherever they sent me: suburban Mt. Juliet, Lebanon, and Springfield; small towns like Lafayette and large Nashville high schools like Hunter's Lane and McGavock, the latter near the Opryland Hotel and Grand Ole Opry House.

My decade at the Baptist Sunday School Board had mostly been spent in the world of books. Many of these drew colorful portraits of life in other parts of the world: Asia, Africa, the Middle East, and Latin America. I worked on books about cultures and ethnic groups a world away from Paris, Tennessee. The subjects of these many books, over two hundred in my nine-year career, formed a tapestry.

My editorial career was in the rear-view mirror, but the tapestry continued. As time passed, I taught students of many different races, ethnicities, religions, and geographic backgrounds. If I could weave them all together, they would form another bright, shining tapestry of the human family.

My students have come from across Tennessee and the United States as well as the following foreign countries: Canada, Mexico, Venezuela, Columbia, Brazil, Bahamas, Haiti, Dominican Republic, Ghana, Nigeria, South Africa, Malawi, Kenya, Ethiopia, Somalia, Sudan, Egypt, Iran, Iraq, India, Spain, Holland, Poland, Romania, Russia, United Kingdom, Japan, China, Vietnam,

Afghanistan, South Korea, Taiwan, Philippines, and I'm probably forgetting several!

I have had students with an array of skills and talents: actors, musicians, singers, dancers, writers, poets, sculptors, painters, computer "geeks,", chefs, sound engineers, law-enforcement and security people, executives, bankers, teachers, and many more. Most were in school to change the direction of their lives. As their teacher, I found this dynamic and thrilling!

One cold, gray November day in 1997, they told me my services would no longer be needed at MTSU after the term ended! I learned the hard way that adjunct teaching is filled with surprises, but more so at some schools than others.

On a tip from a fellow Vol State instructor, I applied and was hired to teach public speaking at Nashville's Tennessee State University, the state's only public historically-black university. I began the fall semester there in 1998. As of 2012, I am still there.

My department head at TSU, when I was hired in 1998, was a native of Cameroon, Central Africa. He spoke six languages: French and English, both official in that country, and four other ethnic languages. He had worked as a broadcaster in his native land.

I learned more about people of color there than I had in my entire lifetime before 1998. (I am still learning!) One thing I have learned: I do not know as much about persons of African descent as I thought I did! I believe part of this lack of knowledge was from growing up under segregation.

Looking back to our home library in Paris, I remember a few books about outstanding black Americans. For example, Mom had a biography of George Washington Carver, the famous scientist who revolutionized Southern agriculture.

The American literature textbook she used at Grove High School had a brief section about James Weldon Johnson, the author and poet who once lived in Nashville and taught at Fisk University, about a mile from the TSU campus!

But these outstanding African-Americans were few and far between. There are many distinguished black Americans I had never heard of until I became a part-time professor at Tennessee State in 1998. Learning was two way: my students learned from me and I learned from TSU and neighboring Fisk University's treasure house of African-American history and culture.

My acquaintance with this unique heritage did not begin in 1998 when I first stepped onto the TSU campus. As a Peabody student in the 1960s, I took a course called Music and Art. One of the requirements was to visit an art museum. On the approved list was the Van Vechten Gallery at Fisk.

One day I drove to the Fisk campus. I think it was in 1966. I had already worked for the *Tennessean* and covered services at the black churches for Bill Reed, so this experience whetted my appetite, I suppose. I remember being amazed at the small, yet diversified collection at the Van Vechten Gallery. I was to return there several times in the years to come.

All during the 1990s, I played at several churches in Sumner and Davidson Counties (Nashville), including a lengthy return stay at Rayon City Baptist in Old Hickory.

I was on staff there in the spring of 1999 when Dad fell at his assisted-living home in Easley, South Carolina. He died on April 18, and we buried him on Tuesday, the twentieth, the same day as the tragic shootings at Columbine High School in Littleton, Colorado.

In the turmoil of Dad's passing, I resigned at the church. There would be others later, but I needed some time off. I inherited a small estate and we began planning to buy a house. We had lived in a rented duplex in Gallatin since 1992, but by then our lives and jobs were centered in Nashville, except for Vol State.

We began house hunting in an older close-in part of Music City that had held its value through the years. We found a nice house just right for us and were able to buy it. We moved during the Fourth of July weekend. I was actually farther from Vol State but closer to TSU. Life is full of trade-offs!

In 1998, the year before Dad died, my son, Josh, graduated from Nashville's Hillwood High School. For me this was a double blessing. His high-school graduation meant the end of child support. By the time we moved into our house in Nashville in 1999, Josh was a student at the University of Tennessee in Knoxville, following in his grandfather Ben Jobe's footsteps.

My father had majored in business and finance on "the Hill." My son majored in accounting. I proudly attended his graduation, magna cum laude, from UT in December, 2002.

Josh was hired by a large Atlanta accounting firm before his graduation. He served as an intern for this company in 2002 and returned to UT to get his master's, which he received in 2004. He served as a graduate assistant while in graduate school. After his graduation in 2004, Josh moved to Atlanta where he still lives and works as a certified public accountant.

Ironically, Josh's great-grandfather, John Harvey Hall (Mom's father) had been a bookkeeper for a mining company near Mt. Pleasant, Tennessee, until his untimely death from flu and pneumonia at age thirty-five in 1920. My son has an accounting thread via his Jobe lineage.

New Millennium, New Faces

In 2000, a year after we moved to Nashville, I was hired to teach at the Smyrna site of Motlow State Community College. The college leased space in a building of the Tennessee Army National Guard. I continued to teach at Vol State and TSU as well.

On Tuesday morning, September 11, 2001, I was in the classroom when Karen Hudson, our administrative assistant, burst into the room without knocking! Breathlessly, she gasped, "They've hit the World Trade Center and the Pentagon! This is a federal building and they're locking it down! Everyone must leave *now*!"

Classes were cancelled for the rest of the day. On Thursday, when I returned to the Smyrna site, National Guard personnel were checking IDs at the front door.

The college continued to operate but conditions were extremely unsettled. Our entire nation was shocked and terrified by the horrific events of September 11! A new word entered our national vocabulary—*terrorism*!

As the days after the attacks crept slowly by, life attempted to return to the way it had been before, but our world and nation had been changed. Even though Paris, Tennessee, in the 1960s was dealing with the Cold War and civil rights, I never really worried about my personal safety.

From a twenty-first-century perspective, despite racism and small-town provincialism, life in the Paris of my childhood seemed calm and comforting. Of course, it wasn't. But our parents' love covered my sister and me like a warm "security blanket" and made us feel safe. Author Thomas Wolfe wrote, *You Can't Go Home Again.*

In June, 2002, about nine months after the attacks on the World Trade Center and the Pentagon, I had another unexpected encounter with evil. While visiting my son, who was an accounting intern in Atlanta, we went to the Martin Luther King, Jr., National Historical Site. I had wanted to go for several years, and the Atlanta visit to Josh provided the perfect opportunity.

Our trip to the MLK Center contained two surprises: one pleasant and one horrifying. The pleasant surprise was a small statue of Mahatma Gandhi on the walkway to the entrance of the museum. This confirmed a teaching technique I was already using—showing my speech students clips from the classic 1982 film *"Gandhi"* starring Sir Ben Kingsley in the title role.

The museum was showing a special exhibit called "Without Sanctuary"—lynching photography! I had heard about lynching, but I did not know much about it. My son and I walked quietly through the exhibit along with everyone else. The mood was hushed and still.

There were signs asking parents NOT to take their small children through it. The reasons were abundantly clear: photo after photo of black men's bodies hanging from trees. Some had been mutilated and/or set on fire! There were crowds of white people, including some children. Some were smiling! There were even a few ancient postcards of lynchings. (Imagine mailing that to someone!)

The entire exhibit was nightmarish, ghastly, and reeked of madness. Those horrific images stayed with me for a long time. I remember seeing a number of "Dracula" and "Frankenstein" movies at the Capitol Theatre in Paris while growing up. But these images we saw at the MLK Center were not of screen actors, but of real people!

I have seen many photographs of Nazi concentration camps during the Holocaust. This was the only thing to which I could compare these lynching photos. The sickening photographs brought to the surface feelings I had buried deep inside from the 1960s—the assassinations of President Kennedy, his brother Robert, and Dr. Martin Luther King, Jr. I'm glad I saw the lynching photography exhibit, but do not want to repeat the experience!

In 1961, when our family visited New York City on a summer trip, our tour of Manhattan included Chinatown. I bought a little booklet of Chinese proverbs. I particularly remember: "May you live in interesting times."

I'm not sure if this proverb was a blessing or a curse, but the early 2000s seemed to be both! First came the terrorist attacks on September 11, 2001. Second, in August, 2005, Hurricane Katrina devastated New Orleans and large parts of the Gulf Coast.

Katrina's effects were felt nationwide. There were lines of refugees in the Louisiana Superdome and lines of vehicles at gas pumps in Nashville. I remember looking for gas on September 12, the day after the attacks, and finding none!

Then in 2008, the year I finally met Coach Ben face-to- face, the global economy crashed. I was blessed to have a job; many lost theirs. My teaching career was enjoyable, but the schools where I taught did not pay that well, compared to schools in other states. On top of that, many salaries were frozen for years!

Despite the adversity of our "interesting times," I now see teaching as my true calling. I am not in this line of work for the money. But it is rewarding in other, intangible ways. I realize most members of the younger generation have the same fears, hopes, and dreams as I did when I was their age. I am much older, but in many other ways not unlike them!

The difference between happiness and unhappiness, success or failure, joy or despair often comes through perception: how you look at your situation. I have seen students who appeared to be equally gifted and talented, but when push came to shove, the one with the more positive attitude excelled. This is just one of many things students have taught me, and why I love teaching.

I have learned to admire the energy and enthusiasm of many young people for life: something I may have lost along the way before this stage of my life. Teaching college students has allowed me to recapture some of that love. And that, I believe, is one reason why the Lord has me in the classroom.

All the experiences I have had up until 2008, I now believe were providential preparation for meeting and getting to know my friend Coach Ben Jobe, who has a connection with me through events that happened a century and a half ago on a farm in Rutherford County, Tennessee.

I once told him, before we met in person in August, 2008, "I can't wait to see what you look like." (This was before I had a copy of his published biography, which has plenty of photos.)

He replied, "I already know what you look like."

Then he told me about something I had completely forgotten. In the summer of 1999, I took a part-time job to help us through the summer since there were few classes. I sat at a table in an office for hours grading papers! Others sat across from me doing the same thing.

One of my coworkers was a tall, lanky older African-American gentleman who was also a Fisk graduate. He told me with a twinkle in his eye, "I know someone I went to school with who has the same exact name as you!"

One day, he asked if he could take my picture and send it to this other Ben Jobe! I agreed. That's how Coach Ben knew what I looked like before I met him!

A short time after we first met, I asked Coach Ben (tongue in cheek) if he thought I was a "redneck" or a "racist." His answer surprised me!

"Oh, I figured that out a long time ago before I ever met you!"

I begged for an explanation.

"Why do you think we kept the name Jobe?"

Most of my adult life, I have heard white Southerners repeat this well-worn phrase: "The slaves took their master's name."

That's not altogether accurate! If the slave-owner was cruel and sadistic, no way would his slave want to keep the family name. When emancipation came at the end of the Civil War, many ex-slaves took surnames they chose for themselves. Had I been in their shoes, I would have done the same!

Coach Ben was complimenting my great- great-grandfather Elihu Coleman Jobe, (1809–1892). He clarified this with these words: "I believe there was a bond of affection there between your ancestor and mine!"

I, too, am grateful to my ancestor who owned Coach Ben's ancestors—---for treating them well within the context of a cruel and inhuman system. The result: the Jobe slaves kept their master's surname. Without that crucial element of human kindness, this story would never have happened!

In hindsight, it might appear the two Ben Jobes meeting and becoming friends was inevitable, but as my friend Dr. Steve Bond observed: "Either one of you could have walked away at any time and that would have been the end of it!"

I am very grateful both Ben Jobes have chosen to see our cup of friendship as full, rather than empty. Because we do, "my cup overflows" (Psalm 23: 5b). The threads that connect us began a century and a half ago, but they continue to weave us together today in a pattern of friendship.

Part Six:

Cloth of Many Colors

"Do not look at his appearance or at the height of his stature…for man looks at the outward appearance, but the Lord looks at the heart"

(1 Samuel 16:7).

In 2008 when Coach Ben and I first met, the church where I had been staff pianist since 2004 merged with another Southern Baptist congregation in the same part of Nashville. The combined church was called Faith Baptist Church. The former church property was sold to a black congregation.

As part of the new church's worship format, a new minister of music was called and thus began the most interesting chapter in the musical side of my life. I had been playing in churches for years, but only once had been part of a praise band, in the late 1980s in Hermitage.

Mark Thomas joined our church in the fall of 2008. He is a published songwriter, actor, playwright, vocal coach, piano teacher—: you name it! We also have in common The Southern Baptist Theological Seminary in Louisville, Kentucky.

You might think having two pianists would cause problems, but I see it as an advantage. Our praise band features Mark on lead keyboard, plus myself on another keyboard providing the "orchestra" strings and other instrumental effects. I still get to play the prelude and offertory on a large, luscious-sounding baby grand piano! Our praise band also has a drummer, bass player, and sometimes a guitar player. Even Pastor Jerry Jones often plays percussion as well.

Most of the people at Faith Baptist are white, but not all. There is the Sayndee family, originally from Liberia, West Africa. Joyce and her teenaged daughter, Diamond, are both singer/songwriters. Joyce came to Music City for the same reason so many others do: music!

Her latest CD, *"Miracle"*, was showcased in a special concert on the evening of May 16, 2010, just two weeks after the historic Nashville flood. There were a number of guest musicians, many of them Liberian-American from across the country, to share in the praise and worship time. The music and celebrating began at 4:30 p.m.

and lasted until 7:00. It was an unforgettable event in the life of our church.

Several years ago, while we were both employed at Volunteer State Community College in Gallatin, I became friends with Dr. Festus Imasuen, a psychologist. He is a native of Nigeria and a naturalized American citizen.

He graduated from Voorhees College in Denmark, South Carolina and from South Carolina State University in Orangeburg, where Ben Jobe coached basketball in the late 1960s, but years before Festus was a student there.

Festus earned two master's degrees from South Carolina State, one in counseling and another in education. He earned a certificate in management and supervision from Cornell University (in partnership with SC State) and his PhD from Southern California University.

Festus transitioned from Vol State a few years ago to a job with the Department of Family and Children's Services of the State of Tennessee. He also has a private practice in Hermitage, east of Nashville.

Festus and I have lively discussions about many things. He is a fascinating conversationalist and a fine Christian gentleman.

In April, 2006, his father, Solomon, died in Nigeria at the age of ninety-three. Festus invited me to his father's wake-keeping in the banquet room of a local motel. They had to book the banquet room because besides

Festus, there are several other siblings, many of whom also live in the Nashville area. The room was filled with family. They all made me feel welcome!

I was the only "European-American" present. The minister who presided was Dr. Eldo Osaitile, who teaches English at Vol State. I was asked to read some selections from Psalms.

It was a wonderful memorial tribute to Festus's father and I was honored he let me be a part of it. After the Scripture and a short eulogy by Eldo, we sang some hymns. The women who led the singing scolded some of the people, saying, "This is not a sad occasion! It is a celebration of the man's life. No long faces!" We celebrated!

After that, we all ate a sumptuous meal that the women had prepared. I ate some Nigerian recipes for the first time in my life. It took me back to my mission trip to Venezuela in 1988. Wake-keeping is one African tradition Americans would do well to adopt! Through knowing people like these, my threads just keep getting more colorful and fascinating!

Two Ben Jobes

The foreword told how Coach Ben and I first met on the phone in April, 2008, after hearing about each other for years. In August, while he was in town for his Fisk class reunion, Coach Ben Jobe and his Caucasian counterpart finally met in person. I picked him up at his motel near downtown Nashville and we drove out to Smyrna to meet my cousin John Moore for lunch.

After eating, we boarded John's spacious van and drove around the area, looking for where Coach Ben thought his family once lived. We could not find the place, as Smyrna has grown considerably since the 1930s.

John is on the board of directors of the Sam Davis Home. Sam Davis was the son of a prominent Smyrna family who owned a large plantation and many slaves. The two-story columned antebellum home is preserved as a historical landmark and is also a picturesque tourist attraction.

John has persuaded the Sam Davis Museum, which adjoins the "big house," to install a small plaque with a photograph of DeWitt Smith Jobe. He and Davis were in the same unit: Coleman's Scouts. Davis was hanged in Pulaski after his capture. Dee Jobe suffered an even worse fate!

On the property are several restored log cabins. As the hot August sun beat down, Coach Ben and I posed as John snapped a commemorative photo of us standing in front of one of them!

During that weekend, he gave me an autographed copy of his published biography *Staying Ahead of the Posse*. I asked for a few extra copies, donated one each to the libraries at Motlow's Smyrna site and the main library at Volunteer State. I also gave one to a man in the public-relations department at TSU.

Later that month, Coach Ben's employer the New York Knicks sent him to Dakar, Senegal, to conduct a weeklong basketball clinic. Before he left, Ben asked me, "Do you want me to bring you anything?"

"I've never gotten a postcard from Africa!" I said. He sent me one, but waited until he actually landed in New York to mail it.

He told me later it would have taken weeks from Senegal.

The message he wrote said: ""The name Jobe is spelled 'DIOP' here. I'll explain later." Apparently, Jobe is an African name, too. DIOP is the French version!

Coach Ben also lived in Sierra Leone in the early 1960s and coached basketball there, too. He was frequently mistaken for an African in that country and in Senegal in 2008. He was often called a "been-to."

"No," he insisted, "my name is Ben Jobe!"

He was told "been-to" simply means an African who has been outside Africa and is returning to the Mother Continent!

Coach Ben and I do not see each other much because of our respective careers. (We talk on the phone on a regular basis.) However, he came to Nashville in October, 2009 for a basketball game at Fisk. It was a Saturday so I picked him up at his hotel on West End and we went to the game. I do not remember who won but I met some of his friends and all were amazed at our story.

Later, we went out to eat. We both like Chinese food so picking a place was easy. I asked him if he would like to see the "Civil War" chest of drawers in our home that his ancestors had probably made!

Ben said he would so I drove him to our home and showed him the chest. He just looked at it silently for a long time. I cannot imagine what was going through his mind but it was a special moment for both of us. A scene was played out in my home a century and a half in the making! Two threads from the distant past were joined that evening—one from each Jobe family.

In March of 2010, Ben returned to Music City to scout for Knicks talent at the Southeastern Conference

Regional Basketball Tournament, which was held downtown in the Bridgestone Arena.

The Tennessee State Museum, a few blocks from the arena, had a special exhibit commemorating the fiftieth anniversary of the Nashville sit-ins, which began in January and ran through the middle of May. I took Coach Ben to see the exhibit before he needed to be at the Arena for the first game. It was a memorable time for both of us.

Ben's involvement in civil rights began in Nashville with the sit-ins and followed him throughout much of his coaching career. This is well documented in Dan Klores's masterful sports documentary Black Magic, which first aired on ESPN in April, 2008. It was two misdirected phone calls from former players of Coach Ben's afterward that finally brought the two Ben Jobes together.

Walking through this exhibit at the Tennessee State Museum in March, 2010 was a personal journey for both of us, but from different perspectives. Many of the photographs were from Nashville's two daily newspapers. I remember many of these images from my own youth. I was fourteen at the time. All during the spring of 1960, the sit-ins dominated the Nashville media and eventually the national media as well.

I can now see why scenes likes these in our Nashville media fifty years ago generated the powerful emotions they did, even in Paris. The "N—" were getting uppity!

They were forsaking their longstanding place on the bottom of the social order! What was the world coming to?

Hopefully, it was coming to its senses!

It might be tempting to cheer the demise of legal segregation and racism with it. As I write this, America's first African-American president, Barack Obama, sits in the Oval Office. His election to the nation's highest office in November, 2008, was called by some the beginning of a new "post-racial" era.

I beg to differ. I have a lifetime fascination with this subject, first as a product of the Jim Crow South, second as a student of Hitler and the Holocaust, and finally as a student of end-times Bible prophecy. I believe one day when Jesus returns, we will truly have a "post-racial" society. The Bible calls it the millennium, a thousand years where Jesus will rule the nations with a "rod of iron" (Revelation 19:15).

Until that happens, racism will be a fact of life. So will slavery—the ugliest thread of all. If you don't believe me, please keep reading.

Ending Slavery Today

Near the end of spring semester in 2009, a student in one of my Vol State classes made a speech about human trafficking: modern-day slavery. I had heard of this before but, like many other Americans, believed it happened primarily overseas in poor countries. This speech taught the teacher a thing or two!

For example:
* human trafficking is the fastest-growing criminal activity in the world;
* it is illegal in all countries, but nevertheless is spreading rapidly;
* it is found in many parts of the United States, including Nashville and Middle Tennessee!

During his speech, the student projected on our classroom screen the home page of an antihuman-trafficking organization with its headquarters in the Nashville area!

I was intrigued and wrote down the website's address. Later, I contacted the founder and director, Derri Smith.

A few weeks later, we met for lunch at a fast-food place near Rivergate Mall. Derri Smith impressed me with her knowledge about modern-day slavery and her passion to do something about it! I was equally impressed that she did all her work on a volunteer basis!

I had a summer class coming up and I invited her to speak to my students about this modern-day evil. Derri came to my class in July and the students were as shocked as I had been when I first heard about it.

She showed images of children doing backbreaking physical work in all parts of the globe, including young girls forced into the sex trade! Some of the material in her PowerPoint drew audible gasps from students. It is strong stuff, but this subject is no fairy tale! There is no happy ending for millions of slaves worldwide. Only a few survive to escape their captivity and begin a new life.

Since early 2012, End Slavery Tennessee has operated from an office on the campus of Nashville's Trevecca Nazarene University. Derri Smith serves as executive director. The website is: endslaverytn.org.

By 2013, End Slavery Tennessee had outgrown the Trevecca office and in the summer moved to larger offices in Nashville's Metro Center office park. Their staff now included two full-time caseworkers and two other part-time employees.

In the Nashville area, Derri and many volunteers have started all kinds of activities to raise public awareness of human trafficking. Part of this involves colleges. I have invited Derri and, more recently Karen Karpinski, to speak to my speech classes at Volunteer State Community College.

Here's one example of a student whose heart was touched by their message and resolved to do something about it. In the fall of 2009, Jamie Blurton was in one of my classes when Derri and Karen came to speak. She was so moved she contacted Derri and asked what she could do to help.

A local heavy-metal bandleader had written a song called "Stolen" and was planning to produce a music video about modern-day sex slavery. Jamie was cast as one of the victims!

The video was shot during a weekend in November, 2009 at a vacant apartment. I attended the shoot on Saturday. In addition to Jamie, a couple of other students of mine had volunteered to be part of it. One young woman applied makeup to the actors. A young man played one of the traffickers, collecting money from sales!

I stayed several hours to watch them work. It was one of the most dedicated and focused groups of young people I have ever seen. They did a fine job.

In the spring semester of 2010, I invited Karen to speak again to my speech classes at Vol State. At the end of her presentation, she added to its powerful effect by showing the music video "Stolen." My students were mesmerized.

The last shot, a freeze-frame, shows several victims holding signs, which together say: "NO ONE SHOULD BE FOR SALE." Jamie was in the middle, her face streaked with tears and makeup as if she had been beaten! Jamie told me later she broke down and cried after the shooting was over!

Despite her petite size, four feet ten inches, Jamie took part in a big fund-raising event for victims of human trafficking in Chicago on October 2, 2010: Ride for Refuge. Jamie was one of thousands of bike riders who pedaled thirty miles! I was one of her sponsors. She was the eleventh top fundraiser in the Chicago Ride.

Ride for Refuge started in a small Canadian town in 2004 with twenty-five riders, according to Derri Smith. Since then it has grown to include multiple sites in the United States and Canada. The 2010 Ride raised almost a million dollars. The 2011 Ride raised even more. The money is used to aid rescued victims of human trafficking, orphans, refugees, and the homeless.

A similar Ride for Refuge was held October 22, 2011, in Hendersonville, thanks to Jamie's leadership! More than fifty riders in nine teams rode between five and fifteen miles. The Nashville/Hendersonville Ride was one of eight locations in the United States. About $7,600 was raised for End Slavery Tennessee!

Jamie Blurton graduated with honors in May, 2011, including being voted Outstanding Graduate by the faculty. She led a volunteer group for End Slavery Tennessee in Hendersonville beginning in January, 2011. Her interest in abolition began when Derri Smith spoke in my class in fall, 2009!

In the fall of 2011, Jamie entered Union University in Jackson, Tennessee, where she has family, to complete her degree in social work. She graduated in May, 2013. Jamie wants a career fighting human trafficking.

Another young abolitionist I know is Lexie Smith, also a former speech student who volunteered with End Slavery while at Vol State. Lexie transferred to Lee College in Cleveland, Tennessee. She also graduated in May, 2013 and seeks a career fighting human trafficking. These young abolitionists, and many more like them, will help make the world slave free at last!

There are many such organizations to fight human trafficking across the globe. It is entirely fitting that End Slavery Tennessee is based in Music City, USA, where slavery once held sway long ago.

Tragically, it is back. There have been several recent arrests by the Metropolitan Nashville Police of human-trafficking rings. One ring was a mother and her two teenaged children! Not everyone who comes to Nashville wants to get their songs recorded. Some come to buy and sell other human beings!

Shortly after we met in 2009, Derri Smith wrote a short article about me for their online newsletter: "Descendant of Slave Owner Becomes Abolitionist." I have been called many things in my life, but I will always wear the title of "Abolitionist" with pride!

I mailed a printout of Derri's article to Coach Ben and he showed it to several of his friends. While in New York and elsewhere, he has shown the photo of us standing side by side in front of the cabin at the Sam Davis Home in Smyrna that August day in 2008. We are smiling and have our arms around each other: the Jobe brothers—their common threads connected after a century and a half!

Can good come out of bad? Can a curse become a blessing? Can tragedy become victory? In the case of the two Ben Jobes, the answer is a resounding **YES!**

I am proud I finally met Coach Ben Jobe after all these years. I am prouder still that he considers me worthy of his friendship. I do not think our story is unique by any means, but we both believe it is a story worth telling. The common threads of the descendants of a slave and slave owner have finally been woven together in a fabric of freedom.

Top Left/Right: Modern-Day Abolitionist Jamie Blurton/ End Slavery Tennessee Official Logo

Bottom Left: Myself, Jamie Blurton and Pastor Jerry Jones, at Faith Baptist Church, Madison, Tennessee.

Bottom Right: Derri Smith, End Slavery Tennessee founder, Jamie and I.

Photos by John Bass; Flyer by Theresa Richardson

Epilogue:
The Fabric of Freedom

"Those who cannot remember the past are condemned to repeat it."

– George Santayana (1863–1952), American philosopher

My great great-grandfather owned two slaves near Smyrna, Tennessee, until the end of the Civil War: Frank and Scott Jobe. Scott's grandson is Coach Ben Jobe, a famous basketball coach whose life story was told on national television in 2008 in the film *"Black Magic."* I am proud to call him my friend.

Besides teaching speech and music appreciation at the college level, I am also a volunteer abolitionist with End Slavery Tennessee. I sometimes wonder what my ancestor who owned Coach Ben's ancestors would think about that.

Epilogue: The Fabric of Freedom

Coach Ben believes our ancestors got along well enough that his family chose to keep the name Jobe. I'm glad they did or the two of us would never have met. I hope Squire Elihu Coleman Jobe (1809–1892) would have approved of me, his descendant born in 1945, teaching in a Tennessee college classroom about modern-day slavery and how to stop it.

Knowing Coach Ben has helped compensate for the slave-owning part of my family's past. That is probably why I have become a latter-day abolitionist.

In the summer of 2010, while writing the first draft of this book, I had a random conversation with Len Assante, my department chair at Volunteer State Community College. Len contacted Eric Melcher of the college's public- relations department, who interviewed me and Coach Ben (by phone in Montgomery) for an article in an online faculty-staff newsletter.

Coach Ben said this about our friendship:

"Sometimes we get emotional when talking about this. We realize that we're living the dream of Dr. King. Ben and I have lived his dream."

"I have a dream that one day....the sons of former slaves and the sons of former slave owners will be able to sit down together at the table of brotherhood."

Martin Luther King, Jr.
Washington, DC
August 28, 1963

Common Threads

About the Author

On a family trip to the Mississippi Gulf Coast in the summer of 1948, his mother told two-and-a-half- year-old Ben Jobe, "We are in Mississippi."

"Where is Mister Sippy?" he asked.

Ben's love affair with words grew as he did. He has been a journalist, advertising copywriter, commercial music composer and arranger, book copy editor and finally, with this book, an author. A professor since 1994, Ben Jobe teaches speech and music appreciation at three public colleges in the Nashville area. He is staff pianist at his church.

"I was blessed to have two loving, caring parents," he says," but it was my mother who passed on her love of teaching, learning, and the infinite beauty of language—spoken and written."

Growing up in Paris, Tennessee, Ben learned about the two slaves in his pre-Civil War family heritage who also shared the Jobe name. In 2008, he met one of their descendants and the two became friends.

In 2009, the author also learned about the growth of human trafficking—modern-day slavery—in his own city and state, and about End Slavery Tennessee. He has been a volunteer abolitionist with this non-profit organization ever since.

" I hope all readers of *Common Threads*," Ben says, "will take away the knowledge of how much all of us—regardless of our backgrounds—have in common. If we will all work together, we can accomplish so much good. If readers understand this, my book will have succeeded."

Made in the USA
San Bernardino, CA
01 April 2014